Building Your Business with the Blueprint of Heaven

Seeing What Heaven Sees and Making it Happen

By

Dr. Ron M. Horner

Building Your Business with the Blueprint of Heaven

Seeing What Heaven Sees and Making it Happen

By

Dr. Ron M. Horner

LifeSpring International Ministries
PO Box 5847
Pinehurst, North Carolina 28374
www.RonHorner.com

Building Your Business with the Blueprint of Heaven

Seeing What Heaven Sees and Making it Happen

Copyright © 2023 Dr. Ron M. Horner

Scripture is taken from the New King James Version®. Copyright © 1982 by Thomas Nelson. Used by permission. All rights reserved. (Unless otherwise noted.)

Scripture quotations are taken from the Holy Bible, New Living Translation (NLT), copyright ©1996, 2004, 2007, 2013, 2015 by Tyndale House Foundation. Used by permission of Tyndale House Publishers, Inc., Carol Stream, Illinois 60188. All rights reserved.

Scripture quotations marked (TPT) are from The Passion Translation®, Copyright © 2017, 2018 by BroadStreet Publishing Group, LLC. Used by permission. All rights reserved. ThePassionTranslation.com

Scripture quotations marked (Phillips) are from The New Testament in Modern English by J.B Phillips copyright © 1960, 1972 J. B. Phillips. Administered by The Archbishops' Council of the Church of England. Used by Permission.

Scripture marked (THE MIRROR) is taken from The Mirror Study Bible by Francois du Toit. Copyright © 2021 All Rights Reserved. Used by permission of The Author.

Heaven Down™ is a trademark of Heaven Down Business, Inc.

All rights reserved. This book is protected by the copyright laws of the United States of America. This book may not be copied or reprinted for commercial gain or profit. The use of short quotations or occasional page copying for personal, or group study is permitted and encouraged. Permission will be granted upon request.

Requests for bulk sales discounts, editorial permissions, or other information should be addressed to:

LifeSpring Publishing
PO Box 5847
Pinehurst, North Carolina, NC 28374 USA

Additional copies available at www.courtsofheaven.net

ISBN 13 TP: 978-1-953684-37-0
ISBN 13 eBook: 978-1-953684-38-7

Cover Design by Darian Horner Design
(www.darianhorner.com)
Image: 123rf.com #96814278

First Edition: March 2023

10 9 8 7 6 5 4 3 2 1

Printed in the United States of America

All trademarks are the property of their respective owners.

Table of Contents

Acknowledgements i
Characters Mentioned iii
Preface v
Chapter 1 Engaging the Assets of Your Spirit 1
Chapter 2 No Plans for Harm 11
Chapter 3 Revelation of Destiny Scrolls 21
Chapter 4 The Spirit of Excellence 31
Chapter 5 Ordered Steps 37
Chapter 6 How Your Blueprint Might Manifest 45
Chapter 7 The Intimacy Key 53
Chapter 8 Your Heavenly Advisory Team 61
Chapter 9 The Miracle is in Your Mouth 67
Chapter 10 Knowing & Engaging Your Star 73
Chapter 11 Becoming Acquainted with Our Star 81
Chapter 12 Obtaining Your Daily Scroll 93
Chapter 13 Governing from Within Our Star 103
Chapter 14 Consider the Stars 109
Chapter 15 Stepping into Position 113
Chapter 16 Dynamics of Our Arche 123

Chapter 17 The Coming Wealth Transfer 129

Chapter 18 Stewarding the Wealth Transfer 139

Chapter 19 Conclusion: Governing as a Son 147

Appendix A 151

Accessing the Realms of Heaven 151

References 157

About the Author 159

Description 161

Other Books by Dr. Ron M. Horner 163

Acknowledgements

The Heaven Down Business Team has been extremely essential in the development of this book. They saw it in the spirit realm, prayed over it, and called it into the earth. The result is in your hands. Thank you to the HDB Team (both earthly and heavenly).

Thanks to Jeremy Friedman and Stephanie Shearin for the information they contributed to this book. I bless each of you who had a part.

May this book bless nations.

——— · ———

Characters Mentioned

The following characters are mentioned in this book:

Enoch: a man in white from the Old Testament.

Ezekiel: the chief angel over our ministry.

Gloria: a woman in white.

Jeremy: one of our Heaven Down Business team members.

Malcolm: a man in white who instructs us from Heaven.

Phillip: Jeremy's personal angel.

Stephanie: my Executive Assistant.

Wisdom: one of the Seven Spirits of God.

———·———

Preface

A few days before Christmas 2022, the Heaven Down Business Team met to inquire about details for an upcoming conference. In the conversation with our Heavenly Business Advisory Team, they mentioned in some detail the book that was to be released at that conference. You are holding it in your hand. Within four days of that meeting, the book was written. It needed editing, but it was essentially ready. The principles herein will help you as you build upon the dream in your heart. We were told by Heaven that this book would be volume 1 of 3. I expect more revelation will be coming.

Businessmen and women have sought throughout the centuries to build upon the dream in their hearts. Some have been immensely successful with some companies approaching or exceeding a trillion-dollar market value in the last few years. These are amounts that are staggering to think of compared to just fifty years ago.

Some include Judeo-Christian principles in the building of their business, while others have clearly built their empires without regard to God or His principles.

However, these business builders of the last few years who have built immense empires are not the first nor are their empires necessarily the greatest to have ever been built. King Solomon obtained vast wealth as a king and a business consultant. Remember, the Queen of Sheba was one of his many clients who came to consult with him for wisdom in governing and commerce.

Before him, we have the example of Abraham who went from having very little to have an empire that became extremely vast. Even when he gave the best portion to his nephew Lot, the principles he lived by brought great wealth again. This proved that it was the principles, not the location that brought the wealth and success. The principles would work wherever he found himself.

The same is true with the principles in this book. They will work in every culture, among every demographic, and with any person willing to consult with Heaven and follow the instructions they are given.

We often have had our way of business building upside down. We have thought of an idea and asked God to come down and bless it. That is upside down. First, we need to consult Heaven and pull down the idea, concept, or blueprint that God wants us to have. Then, we begin to build according to the principles he directs.

Throughout the Bible we have a concept that is repeated several times. Moses, who was put in charge of the transport of millions of Israelites from Egypt to their promised land was instructed to build a tabernacle in which the people could worship. The phrase, "build it according to the pattern I show you" occurred over and over.[1] (See references in footnote).

That is where our trouble begins. If we have the wrong foundation, the solidity of the structure is always in question. In the area I live in we have very sandy soil. When you build a building, you must dig the footer deeper than you would if you were building on clay. If you don't, over time the weight of the settling building will bring cracks and misalignments to the structure. The doors won't open or close properly, windows may not open or shut and walls may even crack, among other things because we didn't build a solid enough foundation. It is that way in our lives and our businesses. This book will help you understand some of those principles. This is the first of what we foresee as a 3-part series. It will help you begin the process and see the blessing of God unfold in your life and the work of your hands. We need to build on solid foundations.

If you have already begun to build and you sense something is not working well, there is good news! God will do things for you retroactively and help you rebuild your foundation so what you build will not be as the foolish man recorded in the gospels who built his house

---

[1] Exodus 25:40, 26:30, Numbers 8:4, Acts 7:44, Hebrews 8:5

upon the sand. When the winds came, the house collapsed. We don't want that to be your legacy. Let's build it properly.

Chapter 1

Engaging the Assets of Your Spirit

Much of what we know about building a business comes from knowledge based in the Tree of the Knowledge of Good and Evil, or as Francois du Toit calls it, the "Do It Yourself Tree" (or DIY Tree). We learned to do all kinds of things without the help of the Father, Son, Holy Spirit, or anyone else, for that matter. We are told to be a "self-made man or woman." However, that is problematic. It forces us to totally ignore the most significant part of our being.

Since we are made in the image of God we will function best when our lives are in sync with God and what he is doing. He made us with three parts: a spirit—which is the interface with Heaven; a soul—which is the interface with the natural realm; and a body-realm, which helps to provide transportation to the other two realms.

Our body is not designed to be the initial recipient of revelation, nor is our soul. Our spirit is to be the first recipient of revelation, not our soul or body. Revelation intake is a function of our spirit. Living from the DIY Tree does not include the spirit as part of the equation. It only recognizes the soul and body.

You and I are not a soul that lives in a body that happens to have a spirit. We are first, a spirit, which has a soul that lives in a body—an earth suit. Most of us have lived our entire lives with our soul being the dominant functioning realm along with our body. When you are at rest, your soul is still functioning to produce answers and solutions. Solutions come from Heaven—not from the earth. Since they come from Heaven, the first recipient should and will be our spirit. Our spirit will then transmit to our soul what it needs to know to process and implement the solution coming from Heaven. Once the soul finds out it does not have to be running the show, you will be much more at rest.

We have discovered how to make that happen. We speak to our soul and say:

> *Soul, I bless you today. Body, I bless you today. Now, soul, it is time for you to rest. Body, it is time for you to rest also. I call my spirit to come forward to the forefront. I will live predominantly from my spirit today.*

You may have a sensation similar to when you take your car out of neutral and put it into drive. It is usually very subtle, but you will find that you have a greater sensitivity to things of the spirit realm—hence you will be able to hear from Heaven better.

One of our first steps in building our business from the blueprint of Heaven is to attune our spirit to what Heaven is saying to us. Often, the Father has been communicating to us through dreams or thoughts that seem to randomly come into our mind. Many of those thoughts are not random at all—they are quite intentional on the part of the Father. Some who are reading this book have retired from a long career or are in the midst of a transition in life and sense a stirring to start something new. This book is going to help you. Others are many years ahead and have an entrepreneurial bent that needs to find its place of fulfillment. Again, this book is going to help. In the next few chapters, you are going to see information I have written about before, but in a more condensed form.

Currently, I have written nearly thirty books and the revelation I received in the process of writing them is going to help you. The book you are holding in your hands right now was written in a matter of days. I had been in a meeting with the Heaven Down Business Team Regarding an upcoming conference—the one this book was released at. Heaven said to me to simply sit down and begin to type. The download for the book was present, so a few hours later I sat down and began typing. This book is the result.

Some who are reading this have an instruction from Heaven to write books. Others have instruction (or desire) to open a coffee shop, or a boutique, or to start a marketing business. To the writers, please understand the book has already been written in Heaven. You simply need to transcribe it in the earth realm. Understanding this makes it much easier to follow the instruction. It works the same way with those who are building their business—whether you are able to hear or see well in the spirit, or simply "know in your knower." Regardless of where your heart is, God will help you discern the information so you can "get it!"

My Executive Assistant has learned things about perceiving that I believe will help you realize you may have been hearing from Heaven far more than you know. Here is her story:

On my journey with the Father, someone once taught me how to recognize the different ways people perceive things, particularly when it comes to what we refer to as "hearing God."

God created people in four different perceiving segments:

- *Seers*
- *Hearers*
- *Thinkers and*
- *Feelers*

All of us have each of these gifts. We all can perceive in each of these ways, but typically for each person, one method will be more dominant that the others. Every day we hear, we learn, and we can also interact with God.

I'm going to tell a story that will help you identify the predominant way you and others perceive spiritual things. A seer, hearer, feeler, and thinker all worked in the same company. Each one of them was late for work one day. Each had to present themselves before the Human Resources Director about why they were late.

The Thinker

The thinker came in and said, "Hey, there was this wreck on the side of the road. Sorry I'm late, it won't happen again."

The Seer

The seer came in and said, "Well, I got up this morning, got in my car, and went to work. I passed a wreck on the way to work." Then, the Seer describes in detail the horrific nature of the wreck and is done.

The Feeler

The feeler comes in and is emotional about this same wreck, and about the loss of life. They tell the HR Director how they slowed down as they passed the wreck and even wept on the way in and that they might need a minute to compose themselves once they get to their desk, but they won't be late again. It was one of the things that was just out of their control.

The Hearer

The hearer says, "Oh man, I got up late this morning. I got my coffee, sat down for a minute to think about things. Then, I realized, 'Oh my goodness, if I don't get up right this minute, I'm going to be even later. By the time I got to my car, I realized that my shoe was untied. I took a moment to tie my shoe. I got in the car and went down the road and I was thinking about how my shoe had been untied and I need to make sure that doesn't happen again. And then suddenly, I came upon a wreck, and you would not believe the carnage that was going on. And I kept thinking about and hearing this song in my head about how life is short. As I was driving in, I was singing that song. 'Do you want to hear it?' I can sing it for you right now. No? Okay. Well, I'm going to go back to my desk. But you know, it was one of those things that was out of my control. But I'm telling you that that song is still in my head."

Distinctions

You can tell the differences between the seer, the hearer, the thinker, and the feeler. We give ourselves away in our everyday speech. Thinkers will say things like: "Well, I think it should be done this way," and, "I thought about it this way," and "I think you should really handle it this way." **Thinkers will have small bits of information dropped in their spirit by the Lord.** *One word, one thought, but it expands a lot in their own heart and their mind. When thinkers speak with other perceiving types like seers and hearers, they can become exhausted because the seers and hearers give them too much information for their comfort. All they need is one word, phrase or* *sentence, the small details. Yet they understand the full package.*

Seers will give themselves away often by saying things like, "oh, I see," "we'll see," or "you should have seen that!" This person sees pictures in their mind like a movie. Their memories are often viewed like movies as well. They can tell you colors or exactly where they were standing. They know exactly what someone was wearing because they see the picture in their mind.

Feelers will take on the emotions of other people. They also give themselves away through their speech by saying things like, "well, I really feel that it should have been done this way," and "this made me feel this specific way. Feelers will also feel the presence of God as well as their experiences in their physical bodies. And if they are not working right and they take on the emotions of others, that they shouldn't carry, they can become sick easily. Feelers are more sickly than the rest.

A hearer can hear sounds in the spirit. They can hear very explicit long words from the Lord. The Lord will be very careful about explaining things in detail to them. They also can sometimes hear audibly in their ears or in their spirit.

People say, "I can't hear from the Lord." Well, Hearers typically can hear. In their everyday speech, they will be the ones that will explain things the longest. They're also very good listeners. They also may be prone to eavesdropping because they obtain all of their information through auditory senses.

We know that learning styles are affected by the way you perceive things. Hearers find it difficult to sit under the teaching of a thinker because thinkers are very matter of fact. Hearers need more details than thinkers tend to give. Seers can learn under other Seers well because the subject is explained at length to give a complete "picture." Seers are able to learn by doing something.

Hearers learn by writing out things.

Thinkers learn by getting small clips of information.

Feelers take it all on as a learner. And if they're not feeling the emotion, if it's not connecting emotionally with them, it's more difficult for them to learn.

Hopefully, this has helped you understand the distinctions in how we perceive things spiritually. We also have a free course on the subject of "The Four Keys to Hearing God's Voice" that might prove useful to you. Additionally, I wrote a book called *Unlocking Spiritual Seeing*[2] that will help you with your ability to see in the spirit as well as to help you recognize what may have hindered your ability to see clearly in the realm of the spirit. These are valuable assets when it comes to building your business with the blueprint of Heaven, but

---

[2] *Unlocking Spiritual Seeing*, LifeSpring Publishing (2019)

you can still build your business without utilizing these assets. We want to help you to learn to develop these abilities, but if you are struggling, we have trained advocates who can assist you in these areas. To find out more, contact HeavenDownBusiness.com.

———·———

Chapter 2

No Plans for Harm

God has the plans of your life worked out. A popular Scripture can be found in Jeremiah 29:11:

> *For I know the plans (blueprints) I have for you," says the LORD. "They are plans for good and not for disaster, to give you a future and a hope. (Emphasis added)*

However, the disconnect is that we may not believe that promise from our Father. Most of us have been taught that we have a great judgment day coming and until that day, we are unsure of the outcome. Let me set your mind at ease. When Jesus gave His life on the cross, He did not die for you, He died *as* you. He took your place. He took the judgment for all your sin—and you had not even been born—upon Himself so you would not have to experience that judgment. He has forgiven you all your sins. He was simply waiting on you to accept what He did on your behalf.

God is not mad at you. He doesn't consider you a worm. He says you are wonderfully and fearfully made.

Psalms 139:13-18:

^{13} You made all the delicate, inner parts of my body and knit me together in my mother's womb.

^{14} Thank you for making me so wonderfully complex! Your workmanship is marvelous—how well I know it.

^{15} You watched me as I was being formed in utter seclusion, as I was woven together in the dark of the womb. ^{16} You saw me before I was born.

Every day of my life was recorded in your book. Every moment was laid out before a single day had passed.

*^{17} **How precious are your thoughts about me**, O God. They cannot be numbered! ^{18} I can't even count them; they outnumber the grains of sand! And when I wake up, you are still with me!*

We MUST understand that God is not mad at us, He is not against us. He is for us. Paul wrote in Romans 8:31:

*^{31} What then shall we say to these things? **If God is for us, who can be against us?***

^{32} He who did not spare His own Son, but delivered Him up for us all, how shall He not with Him also freely give us all things? (Emphasis added)

Paul goes on to say you are being prayed for constantly—by Jesus—and because of that, NOTHING can separate you from His love for you and His plans for you. God loves you immeasurably and there is nothing you can do about it!

Our challenge has been getting past these false conceptions we have had about God, that he really doesn't love us and that things can separate us from Him and we just live until we die.

God already said he has plans for us and these plans are written for us. They are written in a scroll. In this book, I am going to take a small amount of liberty and put it into language that you can understand.

Many times, that scroll will appear as a blueprint. We are all familiar with blueprints, so it is an easy adjustment to make—hence, the title of the book, *Building Your Business with the Blueprint of Heaven*.

Let's read about someone who received the plans to do something significant for his homeland, Solomon.

1 Chronicles 28:9-20:

> *[9] "As for you, my son Solomon, know the God of your father, and serve Him with a loyal heart and with a willing mind; for the LORD searches all hearts and understands all the intent of the thoughts. **If you seek Him, He will be found by you;** but if you forsake Him, He will cast you off forever.*
>
> *[10] Consider now, for the LORD has **chosen you to build a house** for the sanctuary; be strong, and do it."*

¹¹ **Then David gave his son Solomon the plans for the vestibule, its houses, its treasuries, its upper chambers, its inner chambers, and the place of the mercy seat;** *¹²* **and the plans** *for all that he had* **by the Spirit***, of the courts of the house of the LORD, of all the chambers all around, of the treasuries of the house of God, and of the treasuries for the dedicated things; ¹³ also for the division of the priests and the Levites, for all the work of the service of the house of the LORD, and for all the articles of service in the house of the LORD.*

¹⁴ He gave gold by weight for things of gold, for all articles used in every kind of service; also silver for all articles of silver by weight, for all articles used in every kind of service; ¹⁵ the weight for the lampstands of gold, and their lamps of gold, by weight for each lampstand and its lamps; for the lampstands of silver by weight, for the lampstand and its lamps, according to the use of each lampstand. ¹⁶ And by weight he gave gold for the tables of the showbread, for each table, and silver for the tables of silver; ¹⁷ also pure gold for the forks, the basins, the pitchers of pure gold, and the golden bowls—he gave gold by weight for every bowl; and for the silver bowls, silver by weight for every bowl; ¹⁸ and refined gold by weight for the altar of incense, and for the construction of the chariot, that is, the gold cherubim that spread their wings and overshadowed the ark of the covenant of the LORD.

> [19] "All this," said David, "the **LORD made me understand in writing**, by His hand upon me, all the works of these plans."
>
> [20] And David said to his son Solomon, "Be strong and of good courage, and do it; do not fear nor be dismayed, for the LORD God—my God—will be with you. **He will not leave you nor forsake you, until you have finished all the work for the service of the house of the LORD.** (Emphasis added.)

An amazing amount of detail was in those plans. This building was so massive that it took 7 years to complete it. Many times, the significant things we do with our life will take a considerable amount of time.

I remember the story of a man who was 30 years old. He was considering becoming a medical doctor but discovered that it would take ten years for him to finish his education and become a doctor. He complained to a minister that he was 30 years old now, but would be 40 years old when he finished. The minister wisely asked him, "Well, how old will you be in ten years if you don't do this?" Significant things usually take a while to come to pass.

In the passage we just read, we find that was first instructed to know God for himself. God doesn't have grandchildren. He only has children. David described how God knew Solomon's thoughts and understood even the intents of his thoughts. Then David points out that God has chosen Solomon to oversee this massive undertaking.

At that point, the plans were given to Solomon for the temple. This was not a little 10,000 square-foot building, this was a temple.

In verse 12, it says that David gave all these plans that he had received by his spirit. He received them supernaturally. It may be that they came into his spirit as a download and he put the plans from Heaven down on parchment, or oversaw their transmission to parchment by others as they were so massive. David saw every major detail of the structure.

His ability to see the details was a result of his intimacy with the Father. David would often step into a creative mode and play musical instruments and sing. This type of activity often releases stress on our soul and allows creativity to flow into us. We are often able to have new thoughts about something.

In these times, David not only saw the structure itself, but also the personnel that would be needed to manage and maintain the structure as well as perform the various duties needed for the successful operation of the temple.

The details were so intricate that he even knew how much gold would be needed, including the interior design and décor. He knew the details down to the dinnerware and utensils. In verse 18, David describes:

> *"All this the LORD made me **understand in writing, by His hand upon me**, all the works of these plans."*

In Jeremiah 29:11 we read the popular verse:

*I know the plans I have for you to prosper you and not to **harm** you.*

The question we must answer is, "Do we truly believe that God has plans to not harm us?"

How many people do *you* really think believe that?

Many don't believe that because they have been taught to believe that God is mad at them. This is where the court system is so important. People's disbelief in the goodness of God is prevalent. However, through the Courts of Heaven the hearts of people can be established in the understanding that God really does not plan to harm us. It can be established in the earth because it is already established in Heaven. It is already the precedence in His court that He does not intend to harm you. The court system is set up predominantly to not harm.

Visualize this diagram:

See the courts system of Heaven. Below it, see a Consequential Lien[3] with the parameters. Inside those parameters are people. The people believe that God is harming them because of their own sin, or because of bad teaching, but the court system has been set up to prove He is not there to harm.

---

[3] Consequential liens are taught on in the book *Dealing with Trusts and Consequential Liens in the Courts of Heaven*, LifeSpring Publishing (2022).

If you understand a little about the Court System of Heaven[4] you can understand the diagram, but do you believe it?

Since the Father has had this precedence of not harming, why are people still in fear of Him?

Because they don't understand the power of the cross and the work that was done at the cross. Jesus went through a tremendous amount of anguish while on the cross and before. It would help us to realize the weightiness of what He did on the cross. The very act of Jesus' death on the cross is proof that the Father does not want to harm us. That very act was proof for the completion of the knowledge—that we may know He has plans to prosper us and not to harm. Yet, some people believe that if God harmed His own son, so why would He not harm them?

To bridge the gap, we need to see the humanity of Jesus. In the same way that we learn intimacy with the Father, Jesus had to learn it as well. In his humanity, early on in His life, He did not know He would bear the weight of the cross. That is why the struggle was so profound in the garden the night before His death. Jesus, while in the garden, prayed, 'not my will but Yours be done. In His humanity, He made the decision for the sacrifice. We can know that the Father means us no harm

---

[4] I have written several books on the Court System of Heaven. Consult our website: RonHorner.com.

because of that decision to take on the sins of all. Therefore, he has plans to prosper *us* and *not* to harm us.

How do we bridge the gap?

We must put aside all that we think that we know about His humanity. He is the perfect example of building intimacy with the Father. Even as a young boy he was reading and learning the Scriptures. It was an act of his will.

When He was born and put as a human on earth he was veiled from the truth of who he was. He did not know every detail of His future at that point. Do you honestly think that as a child He knew that He would be the sacrifice? He had to grow into that knowledge.

Jesus never sinned, but He was tempted like us. He knew our plight. See Jesus as a little boy pursuing intimacy with the Father. Scriptures tell us He grew in wisdom and stature and in favor with God and men. He had to grow in knowledge and wisdom. It was in intimacy with the Father where He began to know His destiny. He always had a choice. As He walked in His humanity and grew in wisdom and knowledge, He became aware at some point of His destiny that it was the **perfect plan of the Father** for that Scripture:

I have plans to prosper you and not to harm you.

He was the plan. Jesus was the blueprint of the Father for us.

We can stand on that blueprint of His humanity in court and since He became our sacrifice, we can rest—

rest is a governmental position—our governmental position that He is given us through His sacrifice. Jesus is the plan and blueprint with which we can stand. We can trust that Scripture and trust it explicitly. That is for us a righteous verdict and a bond that we can utilize.

> *Father, I ask to step into your Court of Titles and Deeds. I request a bond of Jeremiah 29:11 for the people reading this, for it to be put upon their records. I ask this to be a bond. I ask for it to be a Constructive Trust to be set upon each of their realms, and for the angels to render this righteous verdict as a bond and a constructive trust on behalf of the people in Jesus' mighty name.*

See before you the blueprint the Father has for you and your business. Now stand on it. Let it cover every part of your skin. Wear it like a garment, but it is more than that. It is a part of you. It is trans-dimensional.

> *Thank you, Father, for the plans that you have for us to prosper and not to harm us and to give us a hope for our future.*
>
> *Angels, I commission you to bring all of the blueprints to the people in time and out of time, in every age realm and dimension, for them to be able to step on it and for it to become a part of their being in Jesus' name.*

Chapter 3

Revelation of Destiny Scrolls

Within the pages of Scripture, we find a few descriptions of what we refer to as Destiny Scrolls. Sometimes we see the reference to scrolls like were common in the Biblical era. At other times, they appeared as books and were described in that fashion. In our engagements with Heaven, we also have seen both scrolls and books.

Jeremy Friedman, one of the leaders in the Heaven Down Business Team had been asking for insight from Heaven concerning what many have called "Destiny Scrolls." Heaven responded to his cry for information, and he has allowed me to share this with you:

> *As I stepped into Heaven and accessed the Heaven Down Business Complex,[5] I could see pine trees*

---

[5] In Heaven we have a realm in which we have the Heaven Down Business Complex. It is a spiritual place manned by angels and men in white who assist us in the operation of our business.

like green fencing lining the path to the front entrance. I could sense and feel that I had been here before and was reminded of a dream I had years earlier where I was in Heaven and in this place.

As I stepped into the complex, I was greeted by Gloria, a woman in white assigned to me who greeted me. She remarked that she was happy to see me stepping in for revelation and she reminded me of a book I am to write.

I had asked for clarity and education on scrolls from a scribe and Enoch[6] appeared. He greeted me as we had encountered each other a few times prior and began explaining about different types of scrolls. I stopped him and asked specifically, 'How do we interact and interpret Destiny Scrolls for businesses?'

Destiny Scrolls

Enoch said, 'Destiny Scrolls are the Father's hopes, dreams, and desires for a thing—be it a business, a person, or a ministry. It is the maximum fulfillment of all that entity can be and should aspire to be, it is everything that is good, holy, and pure because it comes from the Father's heart for his children and contains the frequency of love.

---

[6] Enoch is a man in white who did not die. He simply stepped into Heaven and stayed. See Genesis 5:24.

> 'Destiny Scrolls are like guideposts for the saints, they can map out the way Heaven sees a thing and how it could be built out. When following a Destiny Scroll, the best version of something can be achieved because it is the Father's will and His plan for that entity.
>
> 'To interact with a Destiny Scroll, simply peer into it, step into it, and investigate the hidden treasures within.'[7]

[Editor's note: It will help us in our journey to realize that many things we see as just words are far more than that. Many things are living entities that we can interact with and learn from. Our Destiny Scroll is an entity. It is alive and has a voice that can speak to us.]

> As Enoch said this, I could see a series of caves and it was as if I was walking inside one. I could see mounds of gold and gems inside, I could see ideas for inventions,[8] pathways to new schools of thought[9] and tools called the Building Blocks of Destiny.
>
> Asking what those were, I was told, 'These are desires and intentions. When the saints surrender

---

[7] See the chapter on *Ordered Steps*.
[8] Proverbs 8:12 – I wisdom dwell with prudence, and find out knowledge of witty inventions.
[9] Isaiah 55:8-9 – For my thoughts are not your thoughts, neither are your ways my ways, saith the LORD. [9] For as the heavens are higher than the earth, so are my ways higher than your ways, and my thoughts than your thoughts.

their plans and submit their will[10] to the Father, His desire and intention for their lives or business can be made manifest.[11] This is a form of submission and surrender to His divine will. This is the place of laying on the altar and allowing your flesh to be in submission to the spirit—this is spirit first living.

'When you submit to the Father's plans all things will go well and work out for the good of those who love God.[12]

'By contrast, when the saints abandon the opportunity to submit to Heaven's plans and decide upon their own course of action, oftentimes this can divert their ability to cultivate the resources the Destiny Scroll would otherwise yield. The desire and intention of Father's heart is circumvented by the desire of one's own soul. It is this motivation many businesses and individuals follow that can get them into a place that feels fruitless, dry, or empty because it did not have the

---

[10] Romans 12:2 – Stop imitating the ideals and opinions of the culture around you, but be inwardly transformed by the Holy Spirit through a total reformation of how you think. This will empower you to discern God's will as you live a beautiful life, satisfying and perfect in his eyes.

[11] Philippians 2:13 – For it is God which worketh in you both to will and to do of his good pleasure.

[12] Romans 8:28 – And we know that all things work together for good to them that love God, to them who are the called according to his purpose.

grace that was needed for the venture or task at hand.[13]

'Many businesses struggle or fail within the first five years because of this common error.'

I asked, 'By better understanding and following the Destiny Scroll as a guide, our clients' businesses will have better longevity and business outcomes?' I was told that is correct.

I then asked, 'In the event that one is already invested based on the desires of their own soul, how do we get them back on track?'

Gloria laughed and Enoch said, 'That part is easy—just repent and invite the Father back into the business. Take advantage of the simplicity of the Mercy Court[14] *and repent with the clients for where they did not consult or engage Heaven's plan, then go to the Court of Times and Seasons and have their clocks reset. Afterward, deeding the territory of the business to Father*[15] *and inviting him to be the CEO is in good order. Allow the business owners to submit to stewardship*

---

[13] Ephesians 2:10 – For we are his workmanship, created in Christ Jesus unto good works, which God hath before ordained that we should walk in them.

[14] The Mercy Court is one of the Courts of Heaven where we deal with accusation and repentance. See my book, *Four Keys to Dismantling Accusations*, LifeSpring Publishing (2018).

[15] This is accomplished in the Court of Titles & Deeds. See my book, *Engaging the Courts for Ownership and Order*, LifeSpring Publishing (2018).

according to Heaven's plans. These are the best steps to move in the right direction.

'Once this is completed you can go and look at their Destiny Scrolls and help them to discern what the next step is and should be.'

Business Blueprints

I was also shown business blueprints and was told these are quantum maps of how a business will look in any place in time, they can be used in conjunction with the Destiny Scroll to ensure plans are being mapped out and executed correctly.

Commissioning Angels

You may also commission your angels to map out and carry out the plans on the Destiny Scrolls and blueprints to ensure seamless replication of Father's desires for that which you are engaging.

In a subsequent engagement, Jeremy was to learn more.

The Scroll of Life & Times

I was pressing in to hear from Heaven, and I heard Phillip, my angel, speaking, and he said, 'All people are given gifts...some choose to use them to advance the Kingdom (of God), others focus on the world or their personal agenda, but each gift is given by the greatest gift giver of all, God, the Father.

'Gifts are wonderful things but who you choose to use them to serve is most important, will you choose to serve yourself or to serve others? Will you choose to horde them or multiply them?

'Think of the parable of the talents.[16] There were those servants who made wise investments and those who were stingy and lazy and chose not to invest their talents wisely.

'Choose wisely. As you steward the gifts you have been given wisely, more will be given to you.'

I remarked, 'You are not just talking about physical gifting are you?'

Phillip said. 'No, child of God I am talking about the law of stewardship of all things—gifts and resources alike.'

Suddenly, I could see we were in the Throne Room. Before the throne were three chests—one was open while two were closed. I noticed the Sea of Glass like crystal was as a flowing stream, the most beautiful teal blue colored and it was babbling like a brook. As I approached, I heard the Father say, 'Beloved, this is a season of rest for you, it is a season of growth, it is a season of depth

---

[16] Matthew 25:14

of intimacy, and it is a season of preparing the way for what comes next.'

As I heard these words, I could feel an excitement within my heart like I was ready to explode with joy.

As I walked over to the chest in front of me, I peered in the open chest and I saw infant clothes, one blue set, one pink set, onesies, booties, and bonnets. Suddenly, the colors changed to two blue then two pink. I was confused as to the color changing. I asked, 'Father what is the meaning of this?'

He said, 'This part of your scroll had not been written yet.' I was really confused as I believed things to be laid out since the beginning of time, however, I had come to understand that there is a Scroll of Life and Times, which is different from the Scroll of Times and Seasons.

Philip remarked, 'The Scroll of Times and Seasons is the Father's perfect will for our lives and our destinies. The Scroll of Life and Times, however, is a chronology of the choices we make of our own will and the path we choose for ourselves on the earth.

'This is where we have the capacity to make choices that may divert us from the set course Father would have us walk upon. These are the choices we make of self-will, out of our own choosing or our hearts desire.'

I had asked the question, 'Having a vasectomy was not Father's choosing for my life?'

I heard, 'No, my son. That was a choice you chose to make of love and nobility for the one you care for. However, because of that choice, a new timeline has been formed, and you have set course on this new timeline and the former has been nullified.

'The reason why this portion of life and times is unwritten is because your next step or choice is yet unfulfilled.

'The Father's command is always to be fruitful and multiply, therefore He will bless those who choose to do so. He will also bless those whose choice is to not do so, because He loves all of His children and wants for their utmost joy and contentment.'

I asked if this plays into how evil timelines are established and I was told that it is.

I asked how the Destiny Scroll works into the mix and was told the Scrolls of Times and Seasons are just for times or seasons, but the Destiny Scroll is from beginning to end and through all eternity.

I then commissioned my angels to the task of ensuring my life and times line up with my Destiny Scroll and times and seasons by helping me to know the choices to make according to Father's will.

I looked in the chest again and saw the color changing stop on double pink. I heard Father say, 'The choice is yours, but my heart is always for you to be fruitful and multiply.'

———·———

Chapter 4
The Spirit of Excellence

Recalling the story of Noah and how he built the ark, Heaven reiterated to us that excellence was involved. It needed to be water-tight and built with excellence. Thousands of animals would be aboard and plans had to be made to take care of the sanitation issues, feeding issues, and all the details for a long-term stay at the world's first floating bed and breakfast for people AND animals. In the Spirit of Excellence, how many lessons do you think Noah learned?

Those who assisted Noah watched the Spirit of Excellence in operation as Noah cooperated with the Spirit of Excellence day in and day out for an extended period of time. The Spirit of Excellence is not merely a phrase, it is an entity. The Spirit of Excellence is a tangible thing. It can stand. It can speak. Noah let it do both in him.

The Spirit of Excellence stands up. We can ask the Spirit of Excellence to stand up in us as we do the Glory.

Pause a moment and ask for the Glory to stand up in you. Now, ask for the Spirit of Excellence to stand up as well. It will bring a knowing of assurance.

Noah built according to the pattern. The boat was concrete in how it was built, formed, and designed in every way. No matter what happened on the outside, it maintained its existence because of how it was built. Even today, adventurers were able to discover it. The foundation of it was solid.

To take that many years to build something and not give up took the Spirit of Excellence. To do something for that long and have people come against you for years and yet persist until the task was accomplished. Noah did it for years and walked in the concrete, solid knowing and assurance of what was to come. That's how he was able to bear it. It had never rained, and he had never seen rain before, but he built a vessel to float on water for a year and not sink—that required excellence.

Noah maintained the vision *and* the Spirit of Excellence. He continued the vision despite opposition, unbelief, chatter, disbelief, and every demonic force that would come against him because he and his family were the only ones saved in the storm. No one else was deemed worthy because of the demonic activity in their own lives. Today, when we face opposition, we cry like babies.

Noah stood in the Spirit of Excellence—his spirit man stood in the Spirit of Excellence. His spirit became excellent in these things for him to endure. We must call our spirit man to excellence, to walk in it these days.

When we tell our spirit to have the Spirit of Excellence stand up in us, there will be such an assurance of who we are and of who God is. The authority of that so that no matter what, it will produce more than an "it will be OK" type of assurance.

How did Noah walk through this? Obviously, he walked with his spirit forward. He didn't shrink back. With all the external opposition, even with the eight souls with him, there was some extended family that didn't believe.

> *Put your heart and soul into every activity you do, as though you are doing it for the Lord himself and not merely for others. (Colossians 3:23) (TPT)*
>
> *Whatever you do, picture Christ in the person you're doing it for. It makes such a difference when you put your heart into it. (Colossians 3:23) (MIRROR)*

To live contrary to the life of your design is to injure yourself.

In the note to Romans 8:32 (MIRROR), the author wrote, "sin left mankind with an enormous shortfall; grace restores mankind to *excellence*."

Heaven shared a story with us of someone who was in the Roman era, and he was in an arena and was going to be fed to the lions. The Spirit of Excellence he walked in landed him there, but he never wavered.

When you walk in the Spirit of Excellence, you literally will have no fear.

It may have taken us a while to figure out who we are, but it should not take long to figure out that walking in the Spirit of Excellence is the only way to live, even if it means dying. We need to feel the strength and the authority in that. It will matter that we operate our business in the Spirit of Excellence now more than ever.

How long will it take us to walk in this and do this?

Start by doing it every day, a little bit more. We must train just like we train to put our spirit man forward. Just like we train to see in the spirit. The Father wants us to walk in excellence, always. It is a matter of practice.

The Spirit of Excellence is also a being that we can put on. We can step into it, so we become one with it.

"It's a different take on having it stand up inside of us. Yes, we want it inside of us, but then we walk in it. Therefore, we tell it to stand up and we stand in it. We step into it and it just completely envelopes us so that others can't tell the difference between it and us. It's like the goal of the Christian life. Hopefully, we have so much Jesus in us that He is seen and not us. That is excellence.

Are we doing things with excellence and not shipwrecking on a bad day and are we doing it for his glory and not our own? Are we doing our job and doing it well, or are we cutting corners?

If Noah had cut corners because it was taking decades and decades—more than a human lifetime today—to build that ark, that ship may not have lasted as long as it did. They could have had lots of issues because he had all those animals in it. He had to figure out how to keep these animals safe. And if they were mating, then they had babies to deal with. It had to be huge. And they had to store the food for a year, not just for themselves but also for the animals. How did they do the practical stuff? He had to have a lot of wisdom on how to build it according to the plans. If he had cut corners and cheated, it may not have lasted. It might have been a leaky boat, and then everyone was in trouble.

It's the same in our life and business. Cutting corners is a temptation if we don't have integrity or if we don't want to do things with excellence. It may take more time and energy to build a business with Excellence. When we step into that being—the Spirit of Excellence, we become one with it. It is completely on the inside of us, but it also completely covers us.

Building with excellence means you are building to last. We must have the Spirit of Excellence.

Remember, too, Noah was made perfect in his generations,[17] so he had none of the encumbrances from his bloodline, which gave him more room for excellence to stand up.

> *¹ Mirror God; you are his offspring. ² This is how: let the love of Christ be your life; remember how he abandoned himself to us. His love is*

---

[17] Genesis 6:9 – This is the genealogy of Noah. Noah was a just man, perfect in his generations. Noah walked with God.

*contagious, not reluctant but extravagant. Sacrificial love pleases God like the sweet aroma of worship. ³ Love has nothing in common with lust, immoral acts, or greed. The absence of these motives even in the way you talk sets a **standard of excellence**. ⁴ Any distorted language sarcasm or below the belt jokes are uncalled for much rather let gratitude race your conversations. ⁵ The Christ life gives distinct definition to the Kingdom of God. You cannot live a double standard life abusing people through adultery, lust and greed is like worshiping a distorted image of yourself which is what idolatry is all about. (Ephesians 5:1-5) (MIRROR) (Emphasis added)*

The definition of a standard is an agreed way of doing something. Paul is speaking of an agreed way of excellence. A standard is also a banner for claiming possession of something.

Let's step into the Spirit of Excellence today. Let it become one with us and us with him! We are sons who are to live in the Spirit of Excellence.

———·———

Chapter 5
Ordered Steps

My Executive Assistant and I had engaged Heaven and were given instruction concerning how our steps are ordered of the Father.

Not only do we have angels assigned to us and our businesses, we can also learn to co-labor with them to see things accomplished in our lives, business, families, etc. Not only can we co-labor with them, we can also give them instructions concerning certain tasks. Psalm 103:20 tells us that they hearken to the voice of the *dabar*. *Dabar* is a Hebrew word found over a thousand times in the Old Testament. It has multiple meanings. A *dabar* could be a spoken matter, a book, a business, a case, a commandment, a communication, counsel, a decree, a deed, glory, judgment, message, oracle, a word or a work. It has far more possibilities than our typical translations limit us to. This verse tells us that angels hearken—give heed to the Father's business, His judgments, His decrees, His counsel, even the voice of His glory! For us to instruct them to carry out the instructions of the Father is not outside of our purview.

Even though we may have been commissioning our angels to order our steps, we must also be in agreement with the work angels do in the process.

Much has been said and taught about the Seven Mountains of Culture in the Body of Christ. We, as sons of God, are to dominate these various mountains. If our instruction is to establish a coffee shop, we should insist on becoming the very best coffee shop around and one that dominates its particular mountain. Since the desire to establish the coffee shop is in our heart, Psalm 37:4-6, the psalmist wrote:

> *⁴ Take delight in the LORD, and he will give you **your heart's desires**. ⁵ Commit everything you do to the LORD. Trust him, and he will help you. ⁶ He will make your innocence radiate like the dawn, and the justice of your cause will shine like the noonday sun. (NLT) (Emphasis added)*

Our responsibility is to agree with Heaven and be obedient to His instructions.

If we are in agreement with the ordered steps of the Lord, we can conquer whatever is placed before us.

In the Old Testament, when kings conquered an area, they would set about to govern it. We should strive to present excellence in our business. We are conquering the mediocrity that may be present in the marketplace. As we establish a Kingdom business in an area, we are conquering that area for the King. The conquered area has come under the governance of the king who conquered it. That is what *you* will begin to do as you govern your business. We will talk more about that in an upcoming chapter.

---

*If we formulate the conquering,
it becomes a governing.*

To formulate means to methodically create or devise a strategy or a proposal to express an idea in a concise or systematic way. Those are two of the definitions.

If we express the idea of conquering systematically through ordered steps, we will be able to govern.

How can two walk together except they agree? (Amos 3:3)

We should consult Jesus first before we formulate any point or step anywhere on any territory. It must be done via an active agreement because it is an agreement with Jesus.

Seek his will in all you do, and he will show you which path to take. (Proverbs 3:6)

If we acknowledge Jesus in a concisely and systematically, He will direct our paths.

> *When He directs our paths,*
> *then we govern.*
> *We conquer and then we govern.*

Jesus has engineered it to be this way. When something has been engineered, it has been skillfully and deliberately arranged rather than arising naturally or spontaneously. Jesus skillfully and deliberately arranges the agreement. We must have ordered steps that then express in a concise and systematic way how we conquer, then govern.

The steps of the righteous are ordered by the Lord. (Psalm 37:23)

Or

The steps of the God-pursuing ones follow firmly in the footsteps of the Lord, and God delights in every step they take to follow him. (Psalms 37:23) (TPT)

The promise of God to Joshua.

I promise you what I promised Moses: 'Wherever you set foot, you will be on land I have given you.... (Joshua 1:3)

> *Jesus wants to walk on every place*
> *in agreement with us.*

As we follow *His* ordered steps, our steps are ordered as well. We have been busy trying to conquer things ourselves, but the ease is—that He has ordered the steps, but we have to agree with Him.

> *For we are His workmanship, created in Christ Jesus for good works, which God prepared beforehand that we should walk in them. (Ephesians 2:10)*

The Spirit of Excellence

This is where excellence steps in. This is where the Bond of Excellence is important. We can attempt to produce excellence on our own, or we can step into the entity that is the Spirit of Excellence because this is about ordered steps! We must step into the Spirit of Excellence and walk in lock step with Jesus to conquer our mountain.

We are not the initiator of these actions—He is. We simply must agree with the direction He is taking or be sensitive to that direction.

Old Paradigms

This way is a whole lot easier than the old way of taking ground through warfare—the swinging of the swords and all those things. In the past, people would decide to take a territory or a mountain without discerning if they were supposed to do it. Sometimes they weren't prepared to do it, or they weren't strong enough to do it. Sometimes there weren't enough of them to maintain it even if they were successful.

> *Every commandment which I command you today you must be careful to observe, that you may live and multiply, and go in and possess the land of which the LORD swore to your fathers. (Deuteronomy 8:1)*

Many think they can war against principalities using old paradigms and end up with so much backlash that people get hurt. Some have even left the church and given up on intercession because of their experiences of doing things the more difficult way. Jesus modeled the pattern for us:

> *Now I saw Heaven opened, and behold, a white horse. And He who sat on him was called Faithful and True, and in righteousness **He judges and makes war.** (Revelation 19:11)*

We must do the necessary court work to ensure the victory on the battlefield. Many have gone to battle, never having inquired of the Lord for the necessary verdict from the Courts of Heaven.

---
*Jesus understands the process—
court work first, then battlefield work.*

We have found that if we do the proper court work, then the warfare is no longer necessary.

> *How beautiful are the feet of them that bring good news. (Isaiah 52:7)*

Strategized and Ordered Steps

The Father has already strategized and ordered our steps. We need to be in agreement with Him, rather than saying things like, "I don't want to move over there, I don't want to do this, I don't want to do that." These kinds of statements are rebellion. He is saying, "Be yielded to Me, let me bring you into doing what steps I have ordered because Heaven is waiting."

Look at the people that are now being impacted. *He is ordering our steps and all we have to do is agree with it and walk in it* and then see what He does with the beautiful theme of the good news of the gospel of Jesus Christ, and the life-changing messages and revelation that He's given that we don't have to do things a hard way.

---
*If He has ordered our steps
and we come into agreement with it,
He is actually taking the steps, not us!*

That is tremendously freeing. It is not unlike, as a writer, understanding that the book is already written in Heaven and all we have to do is engage with Heaven and get the download. Our steps are ordered, they are already mapped out for us. We don't have to worry and try to come up with a plan. We just need to read the scroll or read the blueprint. Heaven has made it so easy.

In my book on *Engaging Heaven for Trade* is a chapter on *The Golden Pathway*—the map that Heaven has designed for our life. It is laid out before us and all we need to do is live from our spirit and walk it out. If we get off track somewhere along the way, Heaven has provided those in our cloud of witnesses to be working and trading on our behalf to get us back on track. Jeremy was told how some of this work in the chapter on Destiny Scrolls.

In the next chapter, we are going to talk about walking out your Destiny Scroll and stepping into your blueprint.

———·———

Chapter 6
How Your Blueprint Might Manifest

Each person perceives their blueprint just a little differently than the next person; however, there are similarities. I'm going to describe a few to us. If I am speaking to a visual person, and they can utilize their imagination, they will likely have no trouble seeing what appears as a blueprint.

3-D Blueprints

The blueprint may appear, at first, rolled up. It is, by the way, an entity—a living thing. As we engage it, it may come alive.

At times, portions of it will begin to fill out in 3-D fashion like a children's pop-up book. If you have seen the movie, *The Chronicles of Narnia: Voyage of the Dawn Treader*, you may remember the scene where the main characters are in Coriakin's home, and he picks up a scroll and rolls it out on the floor. As he does so, the map on the scroll appears and suddenly becomes alive. This type of scene has been depicted in other movies as well. We have seen similar things in other work we have done in the Courts of Heaven.

Video Blueprints

Sometimes the blueprint will appear as a video that plays out before us. We may only see a short segment of the video, but within that short segment are details we can glean from to build the next step of our business. Often the entire blueprint can appear in video fashion, complete with controls to navigate the video. I have seen them with controls that resemble those on a DVD player. One could stop the video from playing, pause it, back it up, or fast forward. And just like you can do with an image on a smartphone, you can take your thumb and forefinger, place them on the picture and enlarge the image to see details you may not be able to distinguish otherwise. It is remarkable.

I have been able to do that when writing a book. I can back up to review an earlier portion or fast forward to later in the book. I can let the video play or pause as needed to get details that might escape me.

The thing about a scroll is, it doesn't unroll all at once. As you unroll one portion, the last portion will be rolled up and out of view, while the other part of the scroll unrolls to show us something new.

Narrative Blueprints

Some blueprints may appear in a narrative fashion, complete with diagrams and checklists as a roadmap for building your business. Some of how it presents depends upon the person and how they perceive. Those who are more auditory, or knowers, are more likely to experience their blueprints and scrolls in this manner. However, do not determine that any one particular way is the only way you will perceive the information in your scroll.

Ephesians 2:10 tells us that God has ordained things for us to do, and we simply walk them out. He has already written out the scroll of our life and we simply find ourselves walking it out. Remember that He will always require that you use faith regardless of how He delivers the information to you.

Many have struggled with the accusation that they somehow "missed their destiny" by something they did in their life. How do we know that we "missed it." What if it were part of the overall package even if it was a hard thing to live through? It is the bigger picture we need to see. What you have lived through, you can help others through. The secret is to go all the way through it and don't stop in the middle somewhere. Simply keep going, knowing that on the other side of the struggle will be an increased level of the Glory of God in your life. That is what Paul discovered.

> *For our light affliction, which is but for a moment, is working for us a far more exceeding and eternal weight of glory. (2 Corinthians 4:17)*

Remember the story from 2 Chronicles 28 where David received "by the spirit" the download for the building of the temple. He likely received a series of downloads as what he delivered to Solomon, his son, were the details of the building itself, the contents of the building, the personnel who would serve in the building, and more. We only read the overview, but the information was quite extensive.

Remember the story of Noah and his commissioning to build the ark. Remember, it had not rained before, so he did not have that as a baseline. It is doubtful he had seen a ship before, but the Lord spoke to Noah, giving him the information he needed to build it. He was even given the fine details of how to waterproof it. Doubtless, since it took him a long time to build the ark, he had a series of engagements where the Father unveiled the plans and diagrams necessary for completing it.

Remember his predecessor, Adam. Adam had the responsibility of stewarding the Garden of Eden. It was quite expansive and had many components. He was charged with naming the animals. That information probably arose in his spirit as he looked at each animal. He instinctively knew the name of the animal. It simply came forth from within his spirit.

Our spirits are connected to the wisdom that God possesses, and it is likely that Adam received impartations in his engagements with the Father as they walked together in the cool of the day. It was a quiet and peaceful setting conducive to hearing the voice of the Father.

As I noted elsewhere in this book, David would sing and play musical instruments, and get in a creative flow. This would facilitate his ability to tune in to the realms of Heaven. David knew what it was like to access the realms of Heaven and experience Heaven in a way that others of his day did not know.

David experienced receiving counsel in his spirit in the night seasons. In Psalm 16:9 we read,

I will bless the LORD who has given me counsel; my heart also instructs me in the night seasons.

Some of us struggle with sleeping peacefully through the night. Here is a personal practice that I have found works quite well. When I am ready to turn the lights out and go to sleep, I do the following:

I speak to my realms and say,

Body, it is time for you to sleep. Soul, it is time for you to rest. And spirit, it is time for you to access Heaven, check in with my calendar, and do what is scheduled for this evening.

Moments later, I am asleep. My wife will attest to it. Our spirit does not have to sleep, but our body and soul need some recovery time. Your soul doesn't have to sleep but requires periods of rest. However, your body must be allowed to sleep and rejuvenate itself.

Let's keep reading Psalm 16.

*[8] I have set the LORD **always before me**; because He is at my right hand I shall not be moved.*

⁹ Therefore my heart is glad, and my glory rejoices; my flesh also will rest in hope.

¹⁰ For You will not leave my soul in Sheol, nor will You allow Your Holy One to see corruption.

¹¹ You will show me the path of life; in Your presence is fullness of joy; at Your right hand are pleasures forevermore. (Emphasis mine)

David had made the Lord a priority in his life (v. 8). We are doing the same thing by learning to live spirit forward. We are causing our spirit to be the dominant acting realm in our being which comprises a spirit realm, soul realm, and body realm.

As a result of that decision, David said, his heart was glad, and his glory rejoiced. We are carriers of the Glory of God, and as such, the entity of the Glory can reside within us just as Holy Spirit does. As an entity, the Glory can walk, sit, stand, and even talk. In the book of Ezekiel, you can find where the Glory of the Lord stood up (see chapter 3). We can instruct the Glory within us to stand up as well.

¹⁰ For You will not leave my soul in Sheol (hell), nor will You allow Your Holy One to see corruption.

Verse 10 is often thought to speak of Jesus, but David also speaks of us. We are Holy Ones before the Lord. Paul refers to us as saints in his writings. Saints are the sons viewed as holy before the Lord.

David continues to tell us that Heaven will show him the path of life—the Lord would help him unroll his scroll. He also describes that Heaven is filled with joy and pleasures. In all your learning about the blueprint of Heaven, keep the joy in the journey. Have fun with what you are doing. The more somber you get, the more trouble you will have receiving.

The various ways we have seen scrolls and blueprints manifest are just a few ways Heaven can show up and show off. Don't be surprised if the Lord shows it to you in an entirely different way than what you are accustomed to. He can do as He pleases.

Maximizing Your Engagement

A way to maximize engagement with your scroll or blueprint is to become one with it. Here is how we have experienced this. We receive from Heaven the scroll or blueprint. We will refer to the blueprint in this illustration; however, it will work similarly with the scroll.

As a prophetic act, lay the blueprint down in front of you. Remember, it is a living thing. Then step into the blueprint. As you do, you may find yourself immersed in it as if you had stepped into a swimming pool. It will envelop you, and you will feel like it is going into the pores of your skin. Once immersed in your blueprint, begin to look around. Explore what is all around you. Where you need to know more, explore more deeply as if you were scuba diving.

This experience may sound strange, but it is only a portion of how closely we can engage a living thing like our blueprint or our scroll.

Recall that in Chapter 3, on the Revelation of Destiny Scrolls, Jeremy learned the distinction between the Destiny Scroll and the blueprint. As you walk this out, don't be afraid to dive deeper. Heaven wants to unveil so much more to us than we have imagined.

———·———

Chapter 7
The Intimacy Key

Heaven has a team of angels, along with men and women in white who are equipped and ready to help us build according to the blueprint of Heaven. In the Old Testament, we find the story of Moses, who led the children of Israel out of their previous Egyptian bondage. During the forty years it took for the children of Israel to go from Egypt to their promised land—their Canaan, he would periodically get away and ascend Mount Sinai to meet with God. He usually went alone, although on one occasion, he took the 70 elders, Aaron, Nadab, and Abihu. They all had a meal in Heaven with the Father.[18]

Immediately after, the Lord called him to come privately up on the mountain to receive the Ten Commandments. A principle of receiving your scroll/blueprint/book (however you want to refer to it) is knowing God and having an intimate personal

---

[18] Exodus 24:9-11

relationship with Him for yourself. David gave those instructions to Solomon, his son. Moses said similar things to Joshua. Others throughout the Bible understood that it is through intimacy that reproduction occurs.

The Father wants to unveil the particulars of your Destiny Scroll and that process requires that you spend time with Him.

I know of a highly prosperous Australian businessman who went from bankrupt to billionaire in less than fifteen years. A "secret" of his success is that the Lord instructed him to disconnect from his office, his telephone, and other people one day per week. He was to spend that day in total seclusion—whether on a boat on a lake or a hike in the woods—he was to seclude himself, not unlike what David did, and spend time with his heavenly Father. He obeyed that instruction, and his business continued to flourish.

We all need to establish intimacy with the Father, where we give him time regularly, that is His alone. I make it a point to spend time with the Father every day before checking emails, answering the phone, getting on a Zoom call, or anything else. I converse with Heaven, find out what Heaven is saying to me daily before I begin my day in the natural arena.

It is in this solitude and dedicated time before the Father that we can perceive what He is unveiling. He often won't unveil to us when we are a moving target. We need to pause and tune in to what Father is saying through whomever He is using to speak to us at that time.

I never know if I will be conversing with the Father, Jesus, Holy Spirit, one of the men or women in white linen, an angel, or any one of a host of entities that populate the realms of Heaven. I experience this because when I pause to hear from Heaven, I ask the question, "What does Heaven have to say to me today?" Phrasing the question this way allows me to hear from more than one source. They will all be speaking things that edify. They don't compete one with the other. Rather, they are all focused on accomplishing the will of the Father for my life.

The four keys that Mark Virkler talks about in his teaching on *Four Keys to Hearing God's Voice* are:

1. Quiet yourself.

2. Look unto Jesus.

3. Tune to the flow of Heaven.

4. Write down what you hear.

This is explained more in the free online course we have available on CourtsNet.com. We all need to learn how to journal via the Spirit, where we write down what we are hearing, seeing, or perceiving as it flows down from Heaven.

Information from Heaven may come in many forms. It might simply be dropped into your spirit, a random thought going through your mind, or a quickened thought from another person or being. It could be a diagram. There was a man seeking a solution to his desire to provide free and low-cost seminars on praise and worship to small local churches. He was out in the woods bow-hunting when he had an open vision and saw a blueprint that had dropped from Heaven that described a superior hunting bow. He copied the information down before the vision closed. He went on to develop and market the idea, and it became a best-seller in the bow-hunting market. The income off this idea was able to fund his free seminars.

Many ideas come in the form of a dream or vision. There are essentially four types of visions:

Open Vision – the image is seen superimposed over everything else and seems outside of your mind.

Closed Vision – seen within the mind like a TV screen on the inside of your forehead.

Night Vision – Expressed as dreams where we can't consciously interfere with the dream.

Trance – your physical body is suspended, and you are seeing an image or series of images in front of you or within you. Peter fell into a trance while on the rooftop as recorded in the book of Acts.

How visions work is depicted in the movie, *Men in Black 3* where the character has an open vision of a baseball game.

We may not experience any of these types of visions, but you likely have and regularly do experience the form of vision known as a dream. The fact that you can dream prophesies that you *can* see in the realm of the spirit.

Author Blake Healey describes a vision as if you are looking through your car's windshield. You can focus on the bug spots on the windshield, or you can look past them. Often seeing in the spirit works like that for us. Some people are prolific seers, but if your seeing ability is not that well-developed at this time, keep going. Keep pressing in for it to be operational in your life.

Now, back to discussing intimacy with the Father. Often, men struggle with this because they have had no strong role model with whom they could be intimate with. Women who struggle with it often have the same reasons. You can simply ask the Father to heal the wounded places within that are hindering your ability to develop a closeness with the Father.

Developing Intimacy with the Father

1. Find a quiet place free from distractions. Turn your phone on silent or airplane mode, don't look at email, and don't turn on your computer unless you are using it to type in your journaling.

2. Find a consistent time of day. Early morning often works best before you begin thinking about the workday.

3. Call your spirit forward and bless your soul and body but instruct them to relax.

4. Step into your sonship.

5. Step into the Spirit of Excellence.

6. Begin to journal or read the Word. Some people read the Word of God for a few minutes and pray. This isn't so much a time for praying, but for communing with the Father.

7. Just rest in His presence.

8. Invite Heaven to speak to you.

9. Gain your instructions for the day.

10. Follow Heaven's lead.

Pointers

I type what I hear from Heaven. It has advantages for me:

1. I can read what I type. My typing is faster and better than my handwriting.

2. It is easy to recall when Heaven has spoken on a particular topic. I can access that folder on my laptop and search for a specific word or phrase.

3. I have organized my folders, first by year, then within each year I will make folders for each month with a numeric prefix (i.e. 01-January, 02-February, etc.) This way, the folders are in chronological order. During a particular month, I will make the prefix 00-Month for that folder to be at the top of the list.

4. Within each monthly folder, I will name each day's journaling with whatever the date is. (i.e. March 24, 2023).

5. If you aren't using a computer in your journaling but instead are using journal books, cataloging what you receive is more difficult. Use different colored pens or markers to differentiate the things you hear. You also might build an index in the back of the journal book as you go along. Your challenge will be finding a specific thing the Father may have spoken to you months ago. The choice is yours, so have fun!

———·———

Chapter 8
Your Heavenly Advisory Team

If you have read my business books, *Building Your Business from Heaven Down* and *Building Your Business from Heaven Down 2.0*, then you will already understand what I am referring to when I mention a heavenly advisory team.

Religion has falsely led us to believe that God is barely interested in what we do on earth, particularly in business. It has taught us to misbelieve rather than believe. Therefore, we can struggle with things outside our normal range of experience.

If you want to learn leadership principles, you could look at the lives of certain people mentioned in the Bible. Some are great examples of what to do, and a few are great examples of what NOT to do. The Bible records both sides of the story for us—the good *and* the bad.

Once you have acquired your Declaration of Trade and your Deed of Commerce and Trade (which are your basic business documents from the Courts of Heaven) and you establish your trading floor (from which you conduct business), Heaven will introduce you to your heavenly advisory team.

If you still need to acquire your Declaration of Trade or Deed of Commerce and Trade, pause, and visit our website HeavenDownBusiness.com and schedule an Introductory Session so you can begin the process of purposefully getting the validation of Heaven upon your business.

Whether your business has yet to be launched or has been running for some time, Heaven can help us retroactively get your founding documents in order.

Your Heavenly Business Advisory Team

Your business will have a Chief Business Advisor, a Financial Advisor, a Personnel Advisor, a Marketing Advisor, and others. These persons will be men or women in white (saints who have passed on to Heaven before you and now assist businesses in the realms of Heaven.

Your Chief Business Advisor will help guide you through many of the processes your business will go through in its development and expansion. They will work hand in hand with the angels assigned to your business. There is far too much to share in this book concerning these subjects. I recommend you add a few of my books to your reading list: *Engaging Angels in the Realms of Heaven, Commissioning Angels – Volume 1,* and

Engaging Heaven for Trade. They are available from RonHorner.com.

You will want to be well acquainted with your Financial Advisor as he can help you manage your business from the financial side. When we want to know where we stand with our Giving Quotient, we inquire of George (our ministry's Financial Advisor), in the Business Complex of Heaven, and he will help us determine how we are doing. When we need access to funds, again, George helps us with that process.

Heaven has provided us with a personnel department. On earth, we might refer to it as Human Resources, but Heaven pointed out that we don't just have humans on our team. We have angels and a host of entities that work with us.

The Marketing Department includes men or women in white who have expertise that will help you maximize your strategies and efforts in that arena. They will assist you with your website, your marketing efforts, and with knowing who to deal with or who NOT to deal with in some areas. Heaven can give you a heads up which can be very helpful.

A couple of years ago, I was preparing to launch a new book and was planning to do some advertising. My earthly team accessed Heaven with me, and we inquired who on our list of potential parties to advertise with. We also asked who we needed to eliminate to save money, time, and effort. They assisted us in eliminating those who would not be helpful, which allowed us to concentrate on those who would be beneficial to trade with. Heaven knows how to help you maximize your efforts.

Heaven wants you to be a good steward of your resources, and utilizing your heavenly advisory team can help that process. They can assist you in determining the best vendor to use, the ones to avoid, and how to go about the process with them. They may have you pause and wait for an unknown reason. We've experienced this pause which has ended up in us saving money because Heaven knew the product we needed was going on sale in a few days.

At other times, they may know of an updated version of a forthcoming product that will be a better choice for you. Trust the process.

Your Angelic Team

In addition, angels are assigned to your business to help you accomplish everything written for you to do. Depending upon your assignment, you will have any number of angels assigned to you. As you mature in your engagements with them *and* your heavenly advisory team, you may be given even more angels to assist you.

Ezekiel is the name of the chief angel over LifeSpring International Ministries (of which Heaven Down Business is a part). He has several commanders that he oversees, and they, in turn, have charge of many angels. Each of these commanders has oversight over a particular arena of the ministry.

We have learned to engage Ezekiel regularly, and you can and must learn how to engage the angels assigned to your business or ministry on a regular basis. They provide protection, assistance, and far more for us. We can learn to commission[19] them to certain tasks. I have already spoken of this in this book, but you want to be sure to do it.

Commissioning Angels

Here is a sample commission you can use to have your angels read your scroll daily to you. In so doing, your scroll will get deeply into your spirit and will become a motivating force to live by:

I call the angels assigned to (name of the business) to come near. (Wait until you sense their nearness).

In the name of Jesus, I commission you to read my scroll to me daily.

I commission you to unveil my blueprint continuously so that together we might accomplish the design of the Father for (name of the business).

Additionally, I commission you to network with the Chief Angel over LifeSpring International Ministries, Ezekiel, his commanders, and his ranks, as well as Frequency, the Chief Angel over

---

[19] See my book, *Commissioning Angels – Volume 1*, LifeSpring Publishing (2022).

Heaven Down Business, and his commanders and ranks to co-labor in the fulfillment of the Destiny Scrolls for (name of the business).

Additionally, we will ask the angels about the things they need to accomplish their tasks, then request of the Father those items on their behalf. It is a part of our co-laboring with them regarding their work with us.

Any of these angels, men or women in white linen or entities can advise us and teach us. They will not make decisions for us. However, they can point out the pros and cons of a particular course of action so that we make the best possible decision. They can help us see roadblocks or pitfalls in the path that we might not otherwise see. They are invaluable assets to building a business according to the blueprint of Heaven.

In addition, the Father may periodically send Messenger Angels to speak to us on a matter. Because we have viewed angels as weak and puny, we have missed the benefits they bring to us. Some are warring angels, while others are messengers. They are well-equipped for their tasks, and we need to recognize what they bring to the table for our benefit.

As we cooperate with these angels, we are cooperating with Heaven.

Chapter 9

The Miracle is in Your Mouth

Within earshot of you is a miracle. It is not far away. It is not unbelievable; rather, it is quite believable because we have a good Father who loves us and wants the best for us. As a tool, he has given us the ability to receive a language that we can use in prayer that bypasses our mind and comes from our spirit, using our body to talk to Heaven.

It needs to be more utilized when building your business. You may have heard this tool referred to mockingly, or you might have been told it was for a select few (of which you were not a part).

Would we agree that God wants to see our faith built up? Of course, we would.

Look at Jude 20:

> *Beloved, build yourselves up on your most holy faith, praying in the Holy Spirit.*

It would be inconsistent for God to want one person to be able to build up their faith but not another. Some people have taught that speaking in tongues (or praying in the Spirit) is not for everyone. However, we are instructed by Paul in 1 Corinthians 14:39 not to hinder anyone from speaking in tongues. To say that "tongues are not for everybody" is to say that God does not want everyone to be able to build up their faith. That is a ridiculous notion.

Would we agree that God desires us to be edified (built up and encouraged)?

He who speaks in a tongue edifies himself. (1 Corinthians 14:4)

Edifying yourself is a good thing. It means to be built up, encouraged, and strengthened. Aren't there times when we need that? Praying in tongues stirs up our spirit and will positively affect our soul. It seems a good thing to do.

Would we agree that there some things that are mysteries that it would be helpful for us to know?

He who speaks in a tongue does not speak to men but to God, for no one understands him; however, in the spirit he speaks mysteries. (1 Corinthians 14:2)

As we pray in the spirit, understanding of these mysteries can come. These mysteries can be unpacked for us. God is trying to get information *to* you, not keep it from you. As we pray in the spirit, we can also pray in the understanding. It may even come forth in a song.

Advantages of Praying in the Spirit

Praying in the spirit has several advantages for us:

- We are always praying according to the will of God.

- We pray out mysteries and solutions as we allow our spirit to pray.

- Because our spirit is praying, it bypasses the soul and the limitations of your imagination.

- We are edifying ourselves.

- We command angels and direct them where they should go as we pray in the spirit.

- We are co-laboring with our angels to help them coordinate the divine intersections for the appointments God has for our life.

- We are aligning timelines as we pray in the spirit.

- We are building up our faith.

- We are building an edifice for revelation to abide in. Are we building a warehouse or a storage shed by praying in the spirit?

- We are conquering our flesh and teaching our soul submission to the spirit within us.

- We are witnessing a miracle with every syllable coming out of our mouths.

- We are participating in a miracle every time we pray in the spirit. There *IS* a miracle in your mouth.

- We may be averting danger as we pray in the spirit as we mitigate or eliminate a potential situation from occurring.

- Praying in the spirit helps jumpstart our sensitivity to the realm of the spirit.

- It will facilitate our hearing from Heaven more clearly.

- Praying in the spirit helps ensure that things work according to plan.

- As we pray in the spirit, we may produce miracles or pave the way for them to come into our life. God may have a connection in mind that we are unaware of. As we yield ourselves to pray in the spirit, angels will go to work behind the scenes rearranging schedules, adjusting traffic patterns, and giving new thought patterns concerning a matter—all to get us to the right place at the right time.

- Sometimes we are fine-tuning timelines. Each of us has our timeline on which events occur.

Sometimes these events were planned by the Father, while other things were encroachments upon our life by the enemy. Encroachments can cause our timelines to need adjustments so that we can get back to being in lock-step with the plans of the Father.

Some things written in our scroll or blueprint have a degree of flexibility, while others have to happen at a specific time in a certain place. Praying in the spirit helps ensure that things work according to plan.

Cultivating this empowerment in your life will aid you greatly in living out your scroll and blueprint.

At times, you will need to pray intensely in tongues. Often, we will pray softly and quietly, but sometimes you need to put some force behind it. Your spirit may detect obstacles that need to be removed. By praying in the spirit, you activate angels to take care of the situation. Sometimes a little *shimmy, shimmy shoo, shoo* prayer won't do it. *Shimmy, shimmy shoo, shoo* prayers don't move mountains. Strong tongues will.

Sometimes you will want to see your scroll or blueprint but may need help discerning what is in front of you. Praying in the spirit will help remove the fog that is hindering you. At other times, you will pray in the spirit and hear in your mind what you are praying about or journaling.

> *Praying in the spirit is a valuable tool to unlock hidden things.*

Praying in the spirit was kept for the church age, which began on the Day of Pentecost (see Acts 2). God designed it to help propel the church to fully establish the Kingdom of God upon the earth. If you have not stirred your spirit up by praying from your spirit, pause right now and do so. Do it loudly enough that your ears can hear what you are praying. Don't be timid. Break down the walls that have attempted to keep your spirit at bay. Break them down thoroughly!

———·———

Chapter 10

Knowing & Engaging Your Star

Another dynamic I have learned about in my journey will require your spirit to be forward and your soul in a rest mode. It will help you absorb the revelation we are about to share.

As we engaged Heaven, Stephanie and I found ourselves standing on a cliff by the ocean and could see a person down on the beach. As she stepped toward the person, Stephanie was suddenly in front of them. Their back was to us. She described this rugged-looking man with long hair and a long beard. As he slowly turned around, she knew it was Moses because the Scripture came to her about how his face shone with the Glory of the Lord.[20] His face was shining still.

After a few moments of small talk, she began walking with him. As they walked together, Moses held a scroll in his hand and began speaking to a star Stephanie had seen

---

[20] Exodus 34:29

shortly before. He spoke to the star from the scroll, and as he did, the star became enlarged or enhanced.

He explained that everything the Father has us speak from our scrolls enlarges the Kingdom. The scrolls he spoke of in this instance were the daily scrolls attached to this particular star. Each of us has at least one star. Our business will likely have one or more stars. These are heavenly places from which we govern. Each star has a new scroll for each day. We can commission our angels to obtain the scrolls for our star(s) for that day.

We were encouraged to gather the scrolls as they contained the daily outworking of our destiny. As we obtain them and begin to declare the contents of the scroll for the day, details for the day will emerge and align with the plans of the Father outlined in these scrolls. Time encapsulates these measures. We are to agree to the understanding of these things even if they seem challenging to grasp. As we do so, we are co-laboring with Heaven. Gather these scrolls, and as we do, we gather our destiny.

As we do these things, we organize them, co-labor, and work with the angels that would bring the scrolls. It is a *daily* thing for us to do.

We can ask our angels to bring us the scroll for the day and encapsulate the time, reading that scroll.

This is laying our flesh down, which is our soul. We don't do this out of our heads but from our spirits. We are co-laboring with the angels asking for the scroll for the day, stepping into Heaven. We agree with whatever framework Heaven has for the destiny of the day *through time*, trusting the sound of the words we hear. Trusting the sound involves hearing the words and then speaking those words.

Once we have the scroll, as a prophetic act, open it up and hear the sound coming from it because the angels are co-laboring with you. They have given you the scroll for the day. Hear the sound and then speak what you hear.

In our territories and landscapes are stars that were made for us to rule from. As people begin to understand the role the stars play, and as more and more people understand this work and do it, the Kingdom will enlarge bringing about "Thy Kingdom come, Thy will be done."

Engaging Our Star

We received a step-by-step procedure for what we were learning. We discovered that LifeSpring has three stars, plus I have a personal star.

Step-by-Step When Discovering Your Star

1. Request to know your star. Ask to be introduced to your star.

    I ask to be introduced to my star(s).

2. Stand as a son upon your star. A podium may be in front of you for the scrolls to be laid

upon. As a son, you will be clothed in your priestly garments as you begin this.

3. Ask the angels to bring you one scroll for the day for each star. Each star has a scroll. You are to ask for your personal star first.

   I ask for the scroll for my personal star today.

4. Put the scroll in your heart and receive the download of the contents of the scroll.

5. Commit the star to be the Lord's and the Lord's only.

   I commit the star to be the Lord's and the Lord's only.

6. Because the star is a territory, deed it to the Lord.

   I surrender the deed of this star to the Lord of Hosts.

7. Now, read the scroll. If you are unable to discern the contents of the scroll, begin to pray in tongues aloud.

Once you have read the contents of your personal stars' scroll for the day, ask to be introduced to your first business star and then call for the scroll. Commit it to be the Lord's and the Lord's only. Then deed the territory of it to the Lord of Hosts.

Begin to read the contents of that scroll for that day. Continue this process for each of the stars.

Step-by-Step for Working with Your Star Daily

1. Call your spirit forward
2. Step into Heaven
3. Step into your sonship
4. Call the Glory to stand up within you
5. Stand upon your personal star
6. Call for the scroll for your personal star
7. Read the contents of the scroll
8. Repeat this for each star daily

The concept of the stars is throughout Scripture, but like many subjects, we read past them.

First, we must stop doubting what we are hearing:

My darling children, you have nothing to fear; do not doubt for a moment the legitimacy of your sonship! You originate in God and have already conquered the worldly religious system because of the unveiling of Christ in you! His living presence in you is far superior to the futile anti-Christ mindsets present in the world! Their conversation mirrors their source and appeals to a common audience. The pseudo claim of a pseudo system has blindfolded multitudes to believe a lie about themselves. (1 John 4:4) (THE MIRROR)

As we were learning this, Moses gave us a pointer for understanding a subject. We are to call the information forward like a scroll. We did and were pointed to Revelation 12:1:

Suddenly a spectacular symbolic image appears in the sky! A woman clothed in sunlight with a shining moon under her feet and a crown of twelve stars on her head! (THE MIRROR)

Revelation 22:16 tells us:

*I, Jesus, have sent My angel to testify to you these things in the churches. I am the Root and the Offspring of David, the **Bright and Morning Star**. (MIRROR) (Emphasis mine)*

We understood from Moses that we were to do this every morning to help command our day. Job was asked if he had commanded his morning in Job 38:12. We had been learning about governing our realms and territories as well as cultivating our landscape, so this was simply an expansion of what we had been learning.

In 1 Corinthians 15, we find:

[40] There are also celestial bodies and terrestrial bodies; but the glory of the celestial is one, and the glory of the terrestrial is another. [41] There is one glory of the sun, another glory of the moon, and another glory of the stars; for one star differs from another star in glory.

The revelation of stars is all through the Word. 1 Corinthians is a path to the knowledge of stars.

Look at 1 Corinthians 15:40-41 in the Mirror Translation:

> [40] *There are celestial bodies as well as terrestrial bodies. The glory of the one differs from the other. There are skin-bodies and spirit-bodies.* [41] *The glory of the sun differs from the glory of the moon; [while the one radiates light, the other reflects light.] Also, the stars differ from one another. Each one occupies its own unique place in space. (THE MIRROR)*

The path is laid out before us as we read our daily scroll. It enlarges the Kingdom, which is its entire first purpose, and if you are having trouble reading it in your language, praying in tongues will help take care of that.

Praying in the spirit
always brings light.
With every word, what you
are reading will be developed.

This is part of building or governing our territory. We are landscaping it. It is also part of the Trust of Inheritance. This co-laboring is of great value. It is not in and of ourselves but of the Lord. It is *HIS* Kingdom coming. We are each a piece of *HIS* territory.

As people get this revelation knowledge and understanding (and do this with more and more people), it might, at first, look like a jigsaw puzzle of a landscape, but as the pieces are put into place, it fills out the puzzle. It builds out and enlarges the Kingdom.

> *As we take our place as sons,*
> *utilizing this co-laboring with Heaven,*
> *the vastness of everyone being able*
> *to do that on this planet would*
> *bring about the Kingdom quickly.*

Especially if we all did it at the same time—simultaneously.

That is why we pray in the mornings. On planet earth, my morning is in the evening of someone else's day. That being the case throughout the globe, everything is covered, and all times of day are covered—all mornings.

Coupling this information with other information in this book, I could now see the governing attributes of stars that Genesis 1 spoke of. Throughout the Bible are references to stars. We will unpack this more in the next chapter.

Again, governing with the stars is a subject that we probably won't see unless our eyes are open to the concept of it. But once you see it, the repetition of the subject is easily seen in Scripture. More information was to come to help us grasp this revelation and learn to walk in it.

Chapter 11
Becoming Acquainted with Our Star

Stephanie and I had engaged Heaven and were in the upstairs conference room where one wall is clear, and we can see stars and galaxies. Malcolm was with us, and he took what we would think of as a laser pointer pen, pointed to a star far off in the galaxy, and then drew a line to another star. When he did, it created a permanent red line between the stars. Then he did it again to other stars. At first, I thought he was drawing one of the constellations, but that's not what was happening. We wondered why he was pinpointing this particular star in relation to all the others. Some understanding came.

In governance, all stars are relatable to each other.

It doesn't matter what the distance is between them. Our stars are in different places quantumly. In the vision, the second star, which I would have considered to be in a different quantum realm, is a place of *governing in the future.* It looked like our future governance of things **relationally** to how we saw the first elder and John the Baptist.[21]

The first star was Stephanie's personal star, containing her personal landscape and territories, that she could govern. The first star had more of a personal feel.

To Stephanie, it felt like she was governing from the second star. The second star was a governance outside of her personal star on behalf of the Kingdom. To Stephanie, it felt like she was governing from the second star, but her personal star will be in a relational place when she steps dimensionally and quantumly to govern with the other one.

That is why he showed us that it didn't matter how far the stars were apart dimensionally or quantumly. There is a relational aspect to each one of them.

The Bright and Morning Star

Jesus is the Bright and Morning Star. That is where He rules from. That is His governance. *It is a sonship matter.*

---

[21] We had engaged with one of the elders in a prior engagement with Heaven and on another occasion with John the Baptist.

Jesus knows He is God's son and as the Bright and Morning Star rules from that place. He governs from that place.

---

*Do you believe you are
just as much a son as Jesus,
with governance capabilities?*

These are positional matters to the Father.

---

*Take your position as sons,
so that you may govern,
co-laboring with His Word,
His will, His nature—
yes, His very nature.*

Many reflect on their lack of authority in the natural realm, but it is because they are deflecting or reflecting it from that realm. Authority is a governance.

---

*The sons must know
they are sons in order to son.*

It is more than the time and place where we will learn about how we govern; it is the time and place to learn to be sons.

Piercing the Veil of Orphanhood[22]

This revelation will pierce the veil that is the darkness of orphanhood.

Did you know that the word orphan is from the vocabulary of hell? No one—not one, is an orphan. They are sons.

The word "orphan" or "orphan mentality" describes a state people can walk in when they lose their natural parents. This state of mind ends up being an entity that people take on. They are blinded by the *orphanhood,* feeling abandoned by their Heavenly Father or having that feeling because they have lost their natural parents. But Heaven is saying no one—not even one is an orphan.

The Father is calling His sons to stand and to take their places as sons.

It is how the Kingdom of Heaven works—His Kingdom come; His will be done. This is His will. This is His Kingdom.

---

[22] See the prayer template for *Overturning the Curse of the Bastard, Curse of the Eunuch, and Curse of Alienation* at the end of this chapter.

Walking with Wisdom

Then Malcolm sat down, and Wisdom came in and reminded us to invoke her at every turn. In every revelation, invoke her. Wisdom will show the way. She will help illuminate the path.

When we "invoke wisdom," we are invoking Wisdom and all the Seven Spirits of God. It may feel like they are separate, but they are also one.

As an act of faith, we invoked Wisdom and the Seven Spirits and took our stand and position as sons, with our activated stars and where our scrolls were read. We thought of it relationally with the other star in quantum.

> *We thank You, Father, that being a son is much bigger than our minds could ever think or imagine. We thank You. We have had no idea of what has been stolen from us. We have been lied to and told we are orphans and that you have abandoned us. Thank you for the truth.*
>
> *Wisdom, we ask that you illuminate the path in Jesus' name.*

As soon as we asked, the path was illuminated. It ran from the conference room straight out to the star we could see in the distance. As Stephanie stepped off what seemed like a platform and onto the path, she was immediately in front of her star.

Our first step off the platform was to meet the star, even though we had briefly engaged it in a prior engagement. During this day's engagement, our scrolls were read.

We said, "Wisdom, I invoke you at every turn and your revelation. I invoke you and ask that you show me the way. I ask you to illuminate my path and teach me to govern from my stars."

Meeting Our Star

After Stephanie found herself in front of her star, I took a step and suddenly was at one of mine. We each greeted our star (remember, it is an entity, it has sentience.) When Stephanie spoke to her star it responded by saying, "Hello, Stephanie."

I pointed out to her that her star also has a name. She said she would need to sit on that for a minute.

Her star pointed out that humans had not named all the stars. Her star also pointed out that he would also be teaching her how to govern from her star. We learned that stars want to be governed in the morning hours before one's day begins in earnest.

Her star pointed out, "Many stars will come into alignment because of you."

Stephanie added, "When he said, 'you,' he is referring to the position that I'm in with LifeSpring—it has everything to do with LifeSpring Ministries. I would imagine your star is going to say something similar. When he said 'alignment,' it was like a correction in time or something. I see my star, and then I see another star here and another star here and another star here (pointing to different places), and when he said alignment, they all came into the same position together in alignment."

For this revelation to be unpacked and received, we would need the work of Awakening Angels.

I call Awakening Angels to come.

I commission you, Awakening Angels, to go and awaken those that are my family members, my lineage, and those that I will touch in this ministry and through this ministry.

I commission you to awaken the saints to the existence of their stars and the part they play in the governing of realms and dimensions, in the name of Jesus.

We were intuitively learning that one of the purposes of praying in the spirit is when you cannot perceive what is on your scroll, your spirit already knows, and it helps unlock it to us.

Praying in the spirit unveils things for us.

Although our mind may not always perceive it, our spirit will.

It is why the enemy stole speaking in tongues from the church, polluted the knowledge of it, and scared people with it.

> *What a force to be reckoned with if we all prayed in the spirit.*

Remember when Abraham was given the promise about descendants—as many as the sands of the seashore and the *stars* in the sky.

In my book, *Engaging Angels from the Realms of Heaven*, I discuss engaging with our angels to patrol our realms. We then learned about commissioning our angels to specific tasks. Now, we are learning to do more than engage or commission our angels; we are learning to govern the realms we have jurisdiction over and govern territories and stars. These revelations have been progressively unveiled over the last few years. As we engage and co-labor with our angels, Wisdom, and the other Seven Spirits of God, as well as with men and women in white, we will see the Kingdom expanded in our life in new measures. Treasures of revelation and provision will open over our life, and direction and authority will become more apparent and powerful as we walk out being a son living from the Kingdom Dynamics of Heaven.

Prayer Template for Overturning the Curse of the Bastard, Curse of the Eunuch, and Curse of Alienation from the Lord

Father, in the name of Jesus, I request access to Your Courts. I enter in with praise and thanksgiving because You have given me access to these heavenly realms through Jesus. I request access to the Court of Appeals to request the overturning of false verdicts (those established by Satan and Courts of Hell) and the establishment of righteous ones.

I enter today on behalf of _____ (myself, or the name of the person you are praying for) and my (their) bloodline ancestry, all the way back to the hand of the Father.

I confess as sin the activities of my ancestors who engaged in sexual perversion. I confess as sin where these activities became the iniquity of sexual perversion in my bloodline. I repent for those in my bloodline generations who willingly and knowingly, or unwillingly and unknowingly, engaged in adultery, of any form and with any gender in any timeline, in time or out of time, in any age, realm, or dimension, all the way back to the hand of the Father and as far forward as it needs to go.

I confess as sin and repent for selfishness, rebellion, and self-idolatry connected to this sexual sin.

I confess as sin and repent for physical or emotional abandonment of covenant spouses.

I confess as sin and repent for all illegitimate births within the bloodline that gave rise to children and seed falling into the curse of the bastard.

I confess as sin and repent for those who engaged in all fornication, incest, and rape in homosexual or lesbian behaviors.

I confess as sin and repent for those engaged in sexual self-mutilation, or the mutilation of others, and all transgender behavior.

I confess as sin and repent for any who operated in pedophilia and other aberrant sexual conduct of every flavor.

I confess as sin and repent for those in my generations, both in my paternal and maternal bloodlines, who operated in those behaviors and encouraged others to do the same things.

I repent for the originating sin within these bloodlines.

I confess and repent of my own sin in these matters as well.

I agree with You and Your Word about these activities and deeds and confess the sins of my ancestors when they engaged in them. I repent for them on their behalf.

With the intent of my will, I choose to forgive the humans who were and are responsible for introducing this into the family line. I forgive them, bless them, and release them from guilt in the name of Jesus. I ask You to forgive them, too. I ask You to put these sins under the Blood of Jesus in all my family's ancestral bloodlines. I ask for the blood of Jesus to cleanse me and my bloodlines of this sin and these iniquities.

Concerning this sin and iniquity in my bloodline, I request that this Court overturn every false verdict resulting from these sins and iniquities. I request the release of every human captive, with their soul and spirit parts, to be released from these false verdicts and be released from any resulting evil trading floors and evil trade routes, to be granted a righteous judgement based upon my plea for the Blood of Jesus to cover me and my bloodline's ancestors and generations. I ask for the collapse of all evil trading floors and trade routes opened by these ancestral sins.

As an amendment to this case, and in the Court of Cancellations, I am requesting the complete cancellation of the curse of the bastard and the curse of the eunuch for me and my bloodlines and generations. I am requesting the cancellation of the curse of not being allowed into the assembly of the Lord. I enter into this Court my confession and repentance completed just now and on record in the Court of Appeals.

I ask You, Just Judge, to cleanse this curse from me, from my spirit, soul, and body by the washing of the water of the Word, the Living Water, and the Blood of Jesus. I ask You to cleanse this curse and its effects from me and my family line and in me, my generations, and my future generations, as well as from all our DNA. I ask You to release me and all those related to me by blood, marriage, adoption, or civil and religious covenant from these curses and the consequences, impacts, and ramifications of these curses.

I also request restitution to myself and anyone affected by this curse's negative consequences. I request the complete restoration of my spiritual nearness to You, Jesus, and Holy Spirit. I ask that I may worship You in Spirit and Truth from now on. I ask for a verdict of the complete annulment of these curses.

As an amendment to this court case, I request entry into the Presence of the Lord and into the times of His refreshing for myself, my generations, and my future generations.

———·———

Chapter 12
Obtaining Your Daily Scroll

During this engagement with Heaven, we saw something new in the Court of Times and Seasons. We could see a monthly calendar on the wall, and each day had a cubicle in the wall representing it. In each cubicle was a scroll. We were instructed that we could access the Court of Times and Seasons, where we could ask the attendant for one's scroll for their star(s) for that day.

In what we were seeing, the attendant in the Court of Times and Seasons had a sheet of paper (that had come from the scroll) in his hand containing a list of things. On the list, we read, "Night Patrollers, Lasso (but this lasso was big enough to lasso one of the stars we saw), and pipes."

As we continued reading the list, we saw "Verbal Ammunition." This Verbal Ammunition looked like living letters and is used against a natural verbal onslaught. As we requested these things from the Father, the attendant marked them off the list by placing a check mark by each one.

Father, we also request angel food and elixir. We request Night Patrollers, Lassos, Pipes, and Verbal Ammunition for Ezekiel, his commanders, and ranks.

Speaking to the angels, we said,

Now, in the name of Jesus, we commission you to the full use of the Night Patrollers, the Lassos, the Pipes, and the Verbal Ammunition to expand the Kingdom of God, in Jesus' name.

Our personal star and territories are to be governed. Our territories include children and grandchildren, and we can govern their lives from our star. Consider it calling things as if they were.[23]

Speak from your star and call things out, call things in, as if they never were. They are our territories laid on top of theirs as a protective covering. It is an *ordering the day* on their behalf until they get to that place where they can do it on their own, where they walk co-laboring with the angels, but we are going to know this by the reading of the scroll.

Here is a template I use for my personal star:

I bless my spirit, soul, and body, and instruct my soul and body to yield to my spirit this day. I call my spirit forward, in Jesus' name, and I speak to

---

[23] Romans 4:17

the Glory within me to stand up, and I stand in my position as a son of the Most High God. I also step into the Spirit of Excellence this day, and I invite Wisdom and Understanding to walk alongside me today, as well as the others of the Seven Spirits of God. I also call Deep, Revelation, and Unity to walk alongside me.

Then I pray in the spirit for a few moments and continue:

I ask for the scroll to my Personal Star for today.

I declare that the Kingdom of God shall reign this day in all my territories, including my family, my body, and my financial affairs. Peace shall reign, the government of God shall reign, the Counsel of God shall reign, the Wisdom of God shall reign— all the attributes of the Kingdom shall reign, and great shall be the release of the Glory in my territories and the landscape thereof.

We can do this for our children and grandchildren. As we learn to govern these stars via the scrolls, and as the entity Wisdom[24] is present along with Holy Spirit, it will allow us to know how we can do these things without encroaching beyond what we are supposed to. But clearly, we have been given this territory, this help for a reason. It makes sense that our offspring would be on our territories. We immediately put into practice what we were learning and began governing the territory. We

---

[24] Wisdom is an entity (one of the seven spirits of God) that we can ask to walk along side us and help us in our daily lives.

can do this for our children and grandchildren (as well as our spouses). Take a few moments to do the same.

This extends to all my children (I name them), my grandchildren (I name them), my sons-in-law (I name them), and my future sons-in-law.

My children, grandchildren, and sons-in-law shall all fulfill their Destiny Scrolls. They shall have a hunger for God and the things of God. They shall not divert or become lukewarm in their journey but shall arise into their sonship this day.

If I feel a release, I continue:

I ask for the scroll to the LifeSpring Star #1 for today.

I continue praying in the spirit for this arena and declaring certain things in the governance of that star and its territories. Once released in my spirit, I continue to the other stars utilizing a similar pattern.

Governing from one's star is a celestial matter, and although we miss it when reading the Word, Philippians 2 opens the avenue of the celestial. Remember, Philippians 2:10 says,

Every knee would bow of **things above the earth**, *on the earth, and under the earth. (Emphasis added)*

We often just look on this plane with our natural eyes.

Remember Joseph and his coat of many colors. He dreamed about the stars, with the stars representing each of his brothers.[25] The concept of stars is *throughout the Bible.*

I have been given three stars pertaining to LifeSpring that I am to govern in addition to my personal star. Wisdom explained that the first star (my personal star) governs all the other stars. I have been given a territory according to my Destiny Scroll, and I am to do this from my territory and from my governing and rule on my first star (my personal star) as if it is hovering over these other three stars.

We saw vast amounts of wealth in our portion of the business complex. My instruction then came to call in what was needed for the ministry. This may be something you do for your business, as well.

Immediately, I called in a specific amount of money to come into the ministry's bank accounts without delay, in the name of Jesus.

Wisdom said that this is how I was to do it, from my place of governance. I then began to speak in tongues.

Stephanie attempted to describe what she was seeing as I spoke in tongues over my territory, "I see Heaven has opened portals, and treasures are dropping into the portals. Use your lightning bolt![26] Things are falling from the sky."

---

[25] Genesis 37:9
[26] I had been given a lightning bolt as I first engaged with the LifeSpring Star #2.

When Wisdom said, "Call it in," she stood up from her chair, and although she did not remove herself, it was as if the floor became transparent. Then things on the sides of the walls just began to fall through the portals.

"As you began to speak in tongues, treasures, and things that represent treasures such as gold, jewels, and stoles came from the vault through the portal to the earth." Stephanie added, "We request this in time, out of time, and ahead of time, in Jesus' name."

Governing realms, territories, and dimensions are the lot of the sons of God. Isaiah 9:6 foretold this with a passage we typically attribute to only speaking of Jesus.

> *[1] Nevertheless, the gloom will not be upon her who is distressed, as when at first, He lightly esteemed the land of Zebulun and the land of Naphtali, and afterward more heavily oppressed her, by the way of the sea, beyond the Jordan, in Galilee of the Gentiles. [2] The people who walked in darkness have seen a great light (the sons of God arising); those who dwelt in the land of the shadow of death, upon them a light has shined. [3] You have multiplied the nation and increased its joy; they rejoice before you according to the joy of harvest, as men rejoice when they divide the spoil.*

> *[4] For You have broken the yoke of his burden and the staff of his shoulder, the rod of his oppressor, as in the day of Midian. [5] For every warrior's sandal from the noisy battle, and garments rolled in blood, will be used for burning and fuel of fire.*

⁶ For unto us a child (Jesus) is born, unto us a son (the bene *sons of God) is given; and the government will be upon His shoulder. And His name will be called Wonderful, Counselor, Mighty God, Everlasting Father, Prince (Steward/Keeper) of Peace. ⁷ Of the increase of His government and peace there will be no end, upon the throne of David and over His kingdom, to order it and establish it with judgment and justice from that time forward, even forever. The zeal of the Lord of hosts will perform this." (Isaiah 9:1-7) (Emphasis added)*

What we have attributed as only being the work of Jesus in the earth may also include the governing of the sons in the earth. Government is upon our shoulders, not just the shoulders of Jesus. We (along with Jesus) carry a governmental ability. We are the stewards of peace in the earth.

I had heard a vague reference to our personal star from Malcolm (the man in white and our frequent tutor), who had mentioned it on one occasion without explanation.

In Matthew 2:1-2, we read that Jesus had a star—His personal star.

*¹ Now after Jesus was born in Bethlehem of Judea in the days of Herod the king, behold, wise men from the East came to Jerusalem, ² saying, "Where is He who has been born King of the Jews? For we have seen **His** star in the east and have come to worship Him." (Emphasis added)*

This was mentioned several times in the story of His birth.

Paul speaks of the glory (illumination) of one star and that it will differ from the illumination (glory) of another star.[27]

---
*Each star reflects the Glory
its steward carries.*

Much glory brings much illumination.

---
*The glory can be increased
by praying out the scroll of that star—
both in the spirit and in the natural.*

In Revelation 1, Jesus appears with seven stars of the seven churches. Jesus himself had the Morning Star (Revelation 2:28). When it speaks of the stars falling to the earth in Revelation 6:13, it speaks of the authority of that star being no more. It became as dust. The falling to earth of the stars is not a literal falling to the ground as a meteor would do. Stars represent authority, and the seven churches had forfeited the authority.

The woman in Revelation 12:1 appeared with 12 stars representing governmental dominion given to her—essentially by the church by default.

---

[27] 1 Corinthians 15:40

Finally, Jesus is announced as the Bright and Morning Star in Revelations 22:6.

Amos 5:6 refers to a star of a false god. This is repeated several times in the Old Testament. Could this be a concept that is so obvious that we overlook it in our reading of Scripture? It would appear so. The verse quoted earlier from Matthew 2:2 tells us that Jesus had a personal star. If he had more than one star, I do not know. It was significant that Magi from the East came to worship where that star led them.

Abraham was told his descendants would be as numerous as the sand on the seashore and the stars in the skies. Each of us has a personal star.

Stars always have a governmental aspect to them in Scripture.

Malcolm and others have taught us about governing realms, territories, and dimensions. This teaching from Moses brought it even closer to home. He explained that we have a personal star where we are to govern from. LifeSpring has several stars relating to different aspects of our ministry. Not only do each of *us* have a star, we also have territories that we are to govern. We will be learning more about this as we continue.

Chapter 13

Governing from Within Our Star

Just as we have experienced in our many engagements with Heaven, we will start in one place and end up in an entirely different place. Along the way, we learn concepts that build toward the next one. Today was no different. We were in a room with a lot of people. It wasn't hectic, but the air was filled with excitement. Ezekiel was present, showing a mighty beast that had been slain. It was a dragon of some sort, and Ezekiel showed it to this cloud of witnesses. We knew from a prior engagement that he had been warring with a mighty beast, and now he had finalized the victory over it. Ezekiel said, "The mightier they are, the harder they fall." He was standing just a few feet from the dragon with a lasso in his hand that was roped around it's neck.

Would you say that, as a Christian, you've been taught many things that just aren't a hundred percent correct?"

If He who lives inside of you has conquered many things in your life, why have so many put this outside of their understanding when "greater is He, that is in you than he that is in the world"? Simply stating, "He is a Conquering King," and not understanding this concept results in futility. For humanity, co-laboring with the Kingdom within them will cause the slaying of *many* mighty beasts. How odd that we walk the face of the earth mindlessly saying, 'The Kingdom of Heaven is within me.' *He **is** a mighty Conquering King,* and yet, there is no belief in that, no real belief that happens in an individual's life. This is part of *laying down oneself.*

This is part of understanding that you are not doing anything in and of yourselves. You *can* believe that the Lord is slaying your enemies. He *is* preparing a table in the presence of your enemies. This Kingdom Principle is imperative for the sons to walk in new levels of understanding.

How can you walk in quantum if you can't even walk as a son? He *is* the Conquering King. Love conquers all. The mighty beast fell[28] and was slain because of love. It's not just an action; it's a directive. Do you want keys to the kingdom? It starts with love.

The co-laboring of the sons, in love, strengthened the matter to bring this about. Many things on the scroll will be slain, and the weapon is love.

> *Father, I ask for the Supernatural Love to be given to Ezekiel as he co-labors with our angels and of*

---

[28] At the beginning of the engagement Ezekiel, the ministry angel, had slain a mighty beast and brought it forth for us to see.

those that draw near to LifeSpring, for it to be poured out upon them as a directive, as a complete understanding, because it's way beyond what we can think of. It is way beyond what we know.

Father, we ask that we may co-labor and wield the weapon of love.

I also ask for the substance of clarity in this for all, for me, and the truth defender membrane, to be placed upon all of us.

Also, the look and see cream so that our eyes may see.

I ask for the frequency earphones so that we all may hear the frequencies of Heaven and what You are bringing.

Thank You, Father, because I know Your heart is about love, and You showed us that today.

I see your heart for this ministry and what it's doing because this is Your Kingdom. That's why this enemy has been slain. You told us recently that You come against those that come against Your Kingdom work. Thank You.

The Elevation

With the understanding of governing from our star comes an elevation. With new levels comes new warfare, but this level brings new help—help from the Lord. This comes from a new paradigm, from a new place. Because of the elevation, there's extraordinary help. It is a work of the Kingdom.

There is much praying in the spirit regarding these scrolls because, like anything else in our natural mind, you would think we had done it ourselves. This is how we know and can stand in the reality that we are not doing any of this in and of ourselves. These are scrolls *from the Lord* regarding governing territory, not *in and of ourselves*. We completely rely upon these instructions and pray in the spirit regarding our scrolls. When we do our star work, angels are already doing the work we are just beginning to pray about or declare as we are obedient and pray in the spirit regarding our scrolls.

Governing from Within Our Star

As we continued, Heaven wanted to show us something new. We found ourselves on a walkway of light leading us to a large room with no furnishings, just tremendous illumination. Heaven gave us these instructions:

1. Have Wisdom illuminate the path.

2. Govern from rest. This is a part of bringing your spirit forward. In this place (the realms of Heaven),[29] you leave your flesh behind.

---

[29] Isaiah 30:15 "For thus says the Lord GOD, the Holy One of Israel: 'In returning and rest you shall be saved; in quietness and confidence shall be your strength.'"

From here, you can also receive the instruction of the Lord, where you will learn how your scrolls will be received.

Govern from rest.

Once we leave the flesh behind and are truly at that place of stillness, a door opens in front of you, and the path to walk on will be illuminated. As steps are taken, you may feel like you are walking on light, as if that light is going *through* the star that you are walking on.

You may find yourself viewing things from within your star. You are looking *in* the star. Heaven has taught us to look deeper. Looking at the surface of the full star and that light is going through it. Walk *into* it. Walk into the middle of that star—literally into the middle of it. As you walk into the middle of the star, *become* inside of it. Begin to move that star from inside of it, from within that place.

This is the place that we govern from.

This is place that we have deeded over to the Lord. The understanding that we initially governed from above our star is how we started this understanding. Now, we're beginning to understand the **governing from within it**. This is what that's going to look like. Are we putting it (the star) on essentially? Picture the *Iron Man* movie where Robert Downey, Jr. aka Tony Stark, puts on the Iron Man suit and operates from within that suit, from within that environment.

Just like it was depicted with Tony Stark in the movie, the character could steer and go in any direction. From within our star, we ask for *the pathways to the different dimensions.* It's from this place we will do dimensional work—paradigm work. As we govern from within our stars, we will discover much wisdom we need for our businesses. We can learn about different technologies. We can see equations, geometries, and maps. It is from this place that He will teach these secret things.

As a son, step into the illuminated place where we step into rest and stillness. It is from that place that we can access (as we govern from within our star) other dimensions. The Father has placed the ability in each of us to learn differently. Every person is different. But from here, in this place in the realms of Heaven, we will all understand the teaching. Only from Heaven would be given the understanding that all minds could understand.

This is where we will be learning to rule and reign from. Our star is connected to the Bright and Morning Star, which is how we will rule and reign together.

Chapter 14

Consider the Stars

As we engaged Heaven, we found ourselves standing behind Ezekiel, our ministry angel. He turned to us and said, "Consider the stars."

We were looking at a massive star and watching it change colors. It turned from a beautiful red to a golden hue to a bluish-purple.

We asked, "What's happening with this star? How do we consider the stars?"

Ezekiel replied, "All creation is groaning for the sons of men to take their place. SPEAK."

Stephanie remarked, "He wants me to speak to it. Ezekiel, what do I speak specifically?"

Ezekiel explained, "Speak the name above all names."

Stephanie responded, "I speak Jesus. I also speak YHWH."

When she said both of those names, from inside of the star, light came out. Light beams came from all around it.

Ezekiel said, "You are the light in the world. He is the light of the world. This is a navigation point. Consider the stars."

Stephanie remarked, "There's a Scripture we're supposed to understand around 'consider the stars.' Ezekiel, can you help me know what Scripture you want us to speak to the star?"

Ezekiel replied, "This is about speaking the word; the word doesn't return void."[30]

Psalm 8:3-4 came to mind:

³ Look at the splendor of your skies, your creative genius glowing in the heavens. When I gaze at your moon and your stars, mounted like jewels in their settings, I know you are the fascinating artist who fashioned it all! But when I look up and see such wonder and workmanship above, I have to ask you this question: ⁴ Compared to all this cosmic glory, why would you bother with puny, mortal man or be infatuated with Adam's sons? (TPT)

---

[30] Isaiah 55:11 So shall My word be that goes forth from My mouth; It shall not return to Me void, But it shall accomplish what I please, And it shall prosper in the thing for which I sent it.

Ezekiel confirmed that Psalm 8:3-4 was the Scripture he was referring to.

He said, "Read the next Scripture because it's the answer to why you would bother with puny mortal men."

Psalms 8:5-6:

⁵ Yet what honor you have given to men, created only a little lower than Elohim, crowned like kings and queens with glory and magnificence.

⁶ You have delegated to them mastery over all you have made, making everything subservient to their authority, placing earth itself under the feet of your image-bearers. (TPT)

Ezekiel said, "Stop right there. The earth itself is under your feet.

You have stars, and the sons of men are to govern the stars.

"This is placement! This is the understanding of placement and order.

Take your rightful place!

With that, Ezekiel flew off, and our engagement ended.

Chapter 15
Stepping into Position

Heaven has been teaching us several things recently which apply to us personally and in the business arena:

1. To recognize that we are sons.
2. To allow this revelation to revolutionize our way of life.
3. To live spirit forward and not from our soul.
4. To call the Glory of God within us to stand up.
5. To recognize and step into our place as legislative and judicial sons.
6. Begin to rule as a legislative and judicial son.

⁶ For unto us a Child is born, unto us a Son is given; and the government will be upon His shoulder. And His name will be called Wonderful, Counselor, Mighty God, Everlasting Father, Prince of Peace. ⁷ Of the increase of His government and peace there will be no end, upon the throne of David and over His kingdom, to order it and establish it with judgment and justice from that time forward, even forever. The zeal of the Lord of hosts will perform this. (Isaiah 9:6-7)

Our responsibility is to release the government of God in our jurisdiction.

Behold, I give you the authority to trample on serpents and scorpions, and over all the power of the enemy, and nothing shall by any means hurt you. (Luke 10:19)

In the Mirror Bible it reads,

See, I have given you authority to trample upon serpents and scorpions and every powerful symbolic disguise of the enemy. Nothing shall by any means nullify your authentic identity. Your likeness is secured in me. (Luke 10:19) (MIRROR)

Next Steps

- Do not permit lawlessness in your territories (including your business).
- Utilize the angelic forces.
- Commission them to work to release the peace and the Kingdom of God that accompanies the government of God.
- Utilize chaos nets.
- Build the shields.
- Commission the angels to patrol the gates and bridges.

- Remember, the sons *must know* they are sons in order to son!
- Work with the Watchers and Patrollers in your territories.
- Determine if Consequential Liens are involved.[31]

Dominions on Land

Angels use the brown capture bags[32] to capture land that was taken captive by the enemy. It is essentially 'illegal land,' or land under an illegal ownership claim. Unlike the domains which can be captured in the Orange Bag, it is different because this one deals with physical earth. In the situation we saw, it was the result of a consequential lien that a principality put upon a region of land or someone's land that was stolen. When this happens, it can impact your business. This was an encroaching of an evil dominion upon land.

When a consequential lien is placed upon a region of land, an evil dominion is encroaching upon it.

---

[31] Understanding of this can be found in my book, *Dealing with Trusts & Consequential Liens in the Courts of Heaven*, LifeSpring Publishing (2022).

[32] Understanding of this can also be found in my book, *Dealing with Trusts & Consequential Liens in the Courts of Heaven*, LifeSpring Publishing (2022).

We then saw where the bloodshed on it had cursed natural land, and the land had been stolen. The legal right was two-fold—the shedding of innocent blood and the theft of the land. These gave the legal right to the principality to overlay an evil dominion on someone's territory or land mass in the natural realm.

> *We can apply this same information to business arenas where some seem to be "owned" by a certain mindset.*

Remember the account in the book of Daniel about princes being over regions—like the Prince of Persia being over a region that was an entire land mass. It contained a whole body of people. Freedom from the principality is for individuals's and families' sakes. This pertains to land that has been stolen from people, even in the natural. Think of it as the land that the Native Americans had stolen from them. An evil dominion has been placed over them and their heritage—an evil dominion that can be easily captured and dismantled.

Repentance work that has already been done concerning land that has been taken like that can be retaken by simply commissioning the angels to retrieve the land and remove the captured principality. Other repentance work may also be needed. Be led by Holy Spirit in that arena.

The ability to remove the principality is a part of the parameter and will be a helpful tool when dealing with parameters seen on someone's life as a trust. The godly trust in this is all that Heaven has for us, including inheritances that were stolen from us—including land. Apply these principles to your business location(s).

In a vision, we saw an actual natural land mass. We saw a coastline and a castle on a hill overlooking the ocean. We saw the whole land mass captured; then, we saw the evil domain overlaying the captured land mass. This brown capture bag, used in conjunction with removing consequential liens, is to capture the dominion and free the land mass. "Is it that easy to capture the dominion?" we asked Malcolm. "Well, yes! This IS Heaven!" he exclaimed.

Remember, it's only a principality!

Instead of dealing with little peon demons, we are dealing with principalities and getting it over with. We are just now beginning to understand the magnitude of the finished work of Jesus with the simplicity of what we have as sons of God because of His finished work and His shed blood. This is the work of Heaven and the Kingdom Dynamics.

How does this work concerning businesses? There are evil dominions who have taken over business arenas. Remember the Prince of Persia who had overtaken a land mass. As angels are doing this work with the capture bags given to them, it is like what was used by the angel that visited Daniel. That is what was used then and what will be used now—a brown capture bag.

Imagine individual capture bags that are brown and related to the category of business. Imagine looking at each category in the natural and then seeing in the spirit the overlay of the evil dominion over each business category. Now, see the bloodshed that has occurred over them. That is how the dominion can take authority.

One of the first things to look at concerning the legal right a prince exercises is innocent bloodshed, followed by profane worship and all the things you've been taught related to this. That is why that information was the forerunner of understanding this paradigm now.[33]

Begin Repentance

Begin repentance for the shedding of innocent blood and then for profane worship. Follow Heaven's direction concerning other areas of repentance.

Requests for Your Angels

- *I speak to my soul and instruct you to take a step back.*
- *I call my spirit forward now.*
- *I yield to my spirit this day.*
- *I call the Glory of God within me to stand up.*
- *I step into the realms of Heaven.*

---

[33] Taken from *Kingdom Dynamics – Volume 1*, LifeSpring Publishing (2022) & *Dealing with Trusts & Consequential Liens in the Courts of Heaven*, LifeSpring Publishing (2022).

- *I step into my place as a legislative and judicial son.*
- *I step into the Spirit of Excellence.*[34]
- *I call the angels assigned to me to come near.*
- *I request warring angels, backup angels, and others of the Heavenly hosts.*
- *I request for these angels:*
  - *Chaos nets*
  - *Fog dispeller*
  - *Timed devices*
  - *Booby traps*
  - *Bows & Arrows*
  - *Cannons*
  - *Capture bags of every size, color, and dimension, particularly brown capture bags for the capturing of evil dominions.*
  - *Angel food, bread, and elixir.*
  - *Other weapons as designated by Heaven.*
  - *Maps, keys, and the strategies of Heaven.*

Commissioning

I repent for those in league with the workers of darkness seeking to cause chaos and destruction in my territories. I forgive them, bless them, and release them in the name of Jesus Christ.

I request the closure of every portal of hell opened by the sacrifice of innocent bloodshed, pagan worship, and ungodly trades by these persons and

---

[34] This will be unpacked in the next chapter.

those in league with them. I request the cancellation of every trade resulting from the innocent bloodshed through abortion and the sacrifice of children and adults in this nation.

I call my angels near, and request warring angels and backup angels.

I request for you and the other angels of the host, chaos nets, fog dispeller, timed devices, booby traps, bows and arrows, cannons, capture bags of every color, size, and dimension, and purpose, angel food, angel bread, angel elixir, and all other weapons as needed and required to do your duty.

I commission you to the full use of every weapon and strategy in the name of Jesus to successfully establish and maintain peace in my regions, domains, realms, and territories.

I release the lightning of God into my realms, territories, regions, and domains in the name of Jesus Christ.

I commission you to capture every domain and dominion set up by hell and its workers. Bring them into subjection to the feet of Jesus.

I release the peace of God over my city, town, village, county, state, and nation in the name of Jesus, the risen one.

I request the Court of Cancellations to cancel every assignment of hell against those territories under my jurisdiction as a legislative and judicial son.

Declaration

In the name of Jesus Christ, I declare as a legislative and judicial son of God:

The peace of God shall reign over my realms, territories, landscapes, dimensions, city (or town), county (or parish), state, and nation.

There shall be no upheaval, for I govern my jurisdiction by my authority as a son of God.

I say NO to unrest, rioting, destruction, mayhem, and anarchy.

I say NO to "the purge" that has been released upon my nation.

I say, "It shall NOT be! Not on my watch!" It shall quickly come to naught.

There shall be NO expansion of evil in my territories, but my territories shall become a place of delight in the Glory of God.

I stand in my authority as a son and co-reign with Jesus, the risen one with whom I am also risen.

The government of God shall reign this day and in the coming days over my arche, in Jesus' name.

Chaos and other works of darkness shall be shut down entirely in Jesus' name.

There shall be confusion and chaos in the leadership of the agents of darkness seeking to organize this destruction.

Every assignment of hell coming from any counsel of hell of ANY time shall be immediately canceled and thrown down and come to naught in time and out of time and in every dimension. The fowler angels shall completely capture and subdue every foul bird, in Jesus' name.

Every evil spirit shall be brought into captivity.

Every demonic plot shall fail and come to nothing.

Peace SHALL reign and the government of God shall reign in my business because I declare it so, in the name of Jesus Christ, the resurrected one.

Now, pray boldly in the Spirit!

Chapter 16

Dynamics of Our Arche

In this engagement, Stephanie and I were to go to the beach with Malcolm. We walked to and through automatic double doors that opened, leaving the Business Complex, and stepped onto a beach.

Two chairs were on the beach for Stephanie and me, while Malcolm sat on a box facing us. We could see the ocean in front of us. We could hear the waves. We could see the sun and hear the wind and the trees rustling. It was very peaceful. We were told that this was his territory—his landscape.

Malcolm explained, "This is the outer edge of my territory. You are here because you are learning about governing."

We then asked for about *arche* (pronounced *ar-key*[35]). We were pulled back to a bird's eye view and could see

---

[35] The plural is: archai (pronounced *ar ki* with long i

us sitting there with him, but we could see more of his territory and landscape beyond the immediate view.

We saw a library and the place that he had brought us where the whiteboard is. We could see his house—his mansion, and other places in other dimensions. Suddenly, we were back in front of him. We asked, "Malcolm, are these your territories where you rule from and govern?"

Malcolm replied, "It is! Boy, I wish I had known about governing when I walked upon the earth. Things would have been much different. My leadership skills would have been much different. *My destiny now is governing from this place.*"

Stephanie noted, "Malcolm, I understand that you're teaching us a sort of governing."

Malcolm answered, "Yes, I have been entrusted by the Father to bring knowledge for the expansion of the Kingdom of God on earth. It has been part of my redemption.

"The mistakes that I made when I was on earth have been redeemed in Heaven, and now, I can help teach.

"It is all about the goodness of the Father. Do you know the Scripture about how He is strong when you're weak? You are weak when you walk upon the earth, and He is strong. Well, here, He's even stronger. My failures there, He has redeemed. It's part of my story. My *destiny* continues forward here."

We asked, "Would this be considered your *arche*?"

Malcolm replied, **"Your *arche* is your place and your position of authority. It is your territory from which you rule. It is a positional place.**

"When Satan fell, the *arche* that the angels who joined him were in, which was their place—their position, they walked away from it. Your *arche* is an authority. When you realize you are a son, you realize that you have a territory and a landscape, and you govern from there."

We asked, "How is this compared to the Stars?"

He replied, "Your *arche*—your realm of authority has *your stars within it*. The stars are just in a dimension of the realm of our authority, the positional place we will lead from.

The stars are an entity that we must govern.

"You, Ron, have four stars—one personal star and three pertaining to LifeSpring that you govern. One concerns the finances you govern, one concerns the people associated with LifeSpring, and the other concerns the outlets and expansion of LifeSpring. It is very specific about what we will govern, but it's not the whole package. It's not the only thing we use our authority for; it's just a piece. The vastness that you've been shown, is your positional place. I can't even describe it. It's so large. This is part of that as we learn and maneuver."

We replied to Malcolm, "We want to know this concept for the sake of teaching the people and for governing correctly. We want the heart of the Father and what He has for us as we learn and understand this."

He responded, "For instance, as you govern members of your family, and as you learn this, as you walk in this, there is an instant deliverance to come because *that is the heart of the Lord*. That is His heart. His heart is peace and unity and us being able to co-labor with Heaven as these things come to pass in people's lives.

We replied, "Teach us to govern like Jesus taught the disciples. Teach us to govern as Jesus governed. That's what we want."

Malcolm asked, "What season would you say you are in your life?"

Stephanie replied that she was in an interesting season.

Malcolm queried, "What did you learn about patience recently? It's a positional thing, too."

Speaking for both of us, Stephanie said, "Malcolm, I just wanted you to know I'm seated back in this chair in front of this ocean. Whatever it takes for me to expand—to get this, I want it. I don't want to be limited."

He replied, "You aren't limited. You are new." He leaned over and said, "If I were to tell you everything right now, you couldn't handle it. Your body couldn't handle it. Trust the process."

I remarked, "We *are* getting it 'line upon line, precept upon precept, here a little there a little....'

"Well, we say 'yes' to Heaven. We don't want to be limited. Whatever we need to be taught, we ask for the grace for eyes to see and ears to hear."

Malcolm exclaimed, "Now you're governing!"

Governing is submission.

It's such a submissive process.

Malcolm was finished with the lesson, so we got up and walked back inside the building—the LifeSpring Business Complex.

Learning to govern as a businessperson will set you in a stronger position to trade in the earth because you understand that any business idea you have, is for Kingdom expansion purposes. It is not JUST about supporting your family or a few others. It is to have a massive Kingdom impact. Learning and applying these principles will put you ahead of the curve as you build from Heaven down.

———·———

Chapter 17
The Coming Wealth Transfer

Much to do has been given to the various prophecies, messages, and sermons concerning a coming transfer of wealth from the hands of the wicked to the hands of the righteous. However, what has yet to be preached about is the heart's motivation in receiving any degree of wealth transfer.

A central principle of life in the Kingdom involves stewardship. How are we doing when it comes to stewarding the money that is presently coming into our hands? Are we irresponsible? Are we lackadaisical? Are we tight-fisted with what comes into our hands, or are we generous to give to those in need or those persons, ministries, or businesses that Holy Spirit directs us to give to? Do we have a generous heart? Do we have the heart of the Father?

Let me dig a little deeper. What is the first thing you would do if a large sum of money came into your hand? How are you doing when a smaller amount of money comes? Is your first response to be obedient to the tithe or is it to purchase something you have longed for over many years?

Jesus had much to say concerning the motivations of our heart? He also had some things to say about stewardship. Remember the parable of the talents?

Having been in ministry for approximately fifty years, I have had ample opportunity to hear people get excited about "the coming wealth transfer." They shout about how the wealth of the wicked is laid up for the just. However, one of the reasons it is laid up is because the Body of Christ has yet to prove itself to be faithful to what has been placed in its hands. We must own the fact that we have been stewards. We acknowledge that we have treated those who have served us in teaching and preaching poorly. We have believed the old saying, "Lord, keep the preacher humble; we'll keep him poor."

Some have held to the mistaken belief that cheating the laborer out of his just reward was OK. I have pastored in areas where the mindset was that the pastor should do whatever he does for free. They, of course, would not do what they did for free, but that did not matter to them. The is that, even if they gave the pastor everything they had, the pastor would not become rich because of them. They were kidding themselves.

Others have held to the idea of a vow of poverty and do not believe it is scriptural or godly to accumulate wealth. The "wicked" have often been better at stewarding money than Christians.

Heaven has put a lot of emphasis on being a good steward, but we must realistically evaluate how we are doing with our personal stewardship.

I have heard people point to a wealthy unbeliever and say, "Go ahead, make a lot of money because I am going to end up with it!" Do they not realize that what they are saying is tantamount to stealing?

One of the tests of stewardship is our response to the tithe. We want the windows of Heaven open, but we won't return to the Lord of Hosts what rightfully belongs to him. We have been taught wrongly about the tithe in many circles. We have been taught that if we get $1000, that $100 belongs to the Lord...which is true. However, we have misunderstood the way it works. Only the $900 was yours in the first place. The overage: $100 was held in trust by you to return to the Lord as a faithful son. The Father entrusted it to you so that you could strengthen your stewardship quotient. The $900 is YOUR 100%; the extra amount has been placed into your hands (entrusted to you) to help YOU discover your response in handling money.

If the Father can trust you with $100, with $1,000, then He should be able to trust you with millions or billions, but can He? Will it suddenly become too expensive to tithe?

I have heard people agonize over a sizable sum they had received as an inheritance, for instance, and how the amount of the tithe on the increase as several digits in length. It was, in their mind, just so much money!

A preacher had just finished preaching about the tithe and was standing at the door shaking the congregants' hands as they left the service. One old fellow who was not very sharp in the mathematics arena came up to him and said, "Preacher, a tenth is a whole lot. Would a fourth do?"

We have yet to realize that we have been practicing and qualifying for a potential wealth transfer with every dollar increase that comes into your hands.

We also need to learn how to correctly calculate a tithe with our current wage structure, including payroll taxes, Social Security deductions, unemployment deducts, and all the other intricacies of our modern-day systems. When we read about the tithe in Malachi (by the way, just because a Scripture is found in the Old Testament does not mean it is not relevant to us today), we must realize that those Malachi was referring to were living in an agrarian society. Ten percent of what was amassed was not their property if they amassed wages. They were entrusted with returning to the Lord at the storehouse they had been assigned. In today's economy, calculating the tithe is more complex. The simplest way to calculate the tithe is to ask the Human Resources Department where you work (if employed by someone else) what is your actual cost to them as an employee. Employers (in the USA) are required to pay a portion to the government in taxes that matches what the employee pays. You also must consider the other deductions taken from the typical paycheck.

When you can determine the actual cost to the employer of your employment, you will be much closer to knowing the correct amount of money to tithe on.

For example, if one receives $1,000 as their gross weekly salary, a percentage is deducted for a specific type of tax. A matching amount of that particular tax has to be paid by the employer on your behalf; you also have deducted a percentage for Social Security. Additionally, you may receive health benefits as part of your compensation. Those benefits cost your employer on your behalf. That amount is part of your compensation. Then, you also may have contributions to a retirement fund. If the employer matches those amounts, that too is also part of your earnings. They won't benefit the employer; they help you. The simplest way to find the actual amount to tithe is to discover your true cost of employment and work from that number.

People have asked, "Do I tithe on the net or the gross?" The answer is "Neither" because neither the gross nor the net is a true reflection of your earnings. If you have thought you are tithing because you wrote the check based on the gross amount shown on your paystub, you have yet to be tithing because the amount was not a tenth (tithe means tenth) of your true earnings. If you have been attempting to tithe based on the net amount of your paycheck, you have not been giving a qualified tithe. You have been making contributions, but you have not been tithing.

You may have wondered why you were trying to tithe but did not seem to experience the results promised in the Bible concerning the tithe (see Malachi 3), it may simply be because you have been making contributions, but you have not been "tithing." You did not qualify for the benefits because you did not meet the conditions.

What are the benefits?

According to Malachi 3:6-12, we read:

⁶ "For I am the LORD, I do not change; therefore you are not consumed, O sons of Jacob.

⁷ Yet from the days of your fathers you have gone away from My ordinances and have not kept them. Return to Me, and I will return to you," says the LORD of hosts. "But you said, 'In what way shall we return?'

⁸ "Will a man rob God? Yet you have robbed Me! But you say, 'In what way have we robbed You?' In tithes and offerings.

⁹ You are cursed with a curse, for you have robbed Me, even this whole nation.

¹⁰ Bring all the tithes into the storehouse, that there may be food in My house, and try Me now in this," says the LORD of hosts, "If I will not open for you the windows of heaven and pour out for you such blessing that there will not be room enough to receive it.

¹¹ "And I will rebuke the devourer for your sakes, so that he will not destroy the fruit of your ground, nor shall the vine fail to bear fruit for you in the field," says the LORD of hosts;

¹² And all nations will call you blessed, for you will be a delightful land," says the LORD of hosts.

The Israelites were experiencing a disconnect between themselves and God. The source of the disconnect was robbery. The result of that robbery was a curse upon the whole nation. I don't know about you, but I want nothing to do with a curse on my life.

In the goodness of God, he provided the solution in verse 10:

Bring ALL the tithes into the storehouse...not just part of them, but ALL the tithes into the storehouse. A storehouse is where we receive food spiritually. What ministry have you been assigned to? If you have been assigned to a particular body of believers—an ecclesia, your duty is to support that storehouse by your tithes AND offerings. Remember, the Israelites were not just withholding the tithe; they were not giving offerings either. He challenged them to test God in this manner.

You are not giving until AFTER you have tithed!

The result for them would be:

1. He would open Heaven's windows (portals) (Revelation would be released into your life!). I want a revelation flow into my life. How about you?

2. He would pour out for them such blessing that it could not be contained.

3. The Lord of Hosts would rebuke the devourer (seed-eater) for their sake.

4. He would prohibit the seed-eater from destroying the fruits of their ground.

5. He would prohibit their vines from having an aborted or premature harvest that is less than what it should be.

AND...

6. All nations would call them blessed.

7. They would be a delightsome, purpose-filled land—a land that would be enviable by others!

The promises of God to them are His promises to you!

The tithe is a return to the rightful owner that which has been placed in trust to you.

Because it is not always simple to calculate, I add an amount of money above and beyond what would be the tithable amount. Any overage will be an offering to the Lord and into the storehouse to which I am assigned.

Some have been legalistic in their calculation of the tithe writing the amount of their check or online donation down to the penny. That may be how they are wired, but I encourage you to do more than the minimum. The Father enabled you to earn and has blessed the work of your hands.

He who has a generous eye will be blessed, For he gives of his bread to the poor. (Proverbs 22:9)

Given that the best guess of the percentage of tithing believers in the Body of Christ at large is at best, under 20% of all believers, are we ready for a sudden influx of wealth? We have yet to prove ourselves with little; how can we expect to be made rulers of much?

In Luke 16:10, Jesus called out those in His audience by saying:

He who is faithful in what is least is faithful also in much; and he who is unjust in what is least is unjust also in much.

We need to make sure we are faithful with the lesser amounts to prove ourselves trustworthy with the greater. When these concepts are fully implemented in our lives, a wealth transfer can come. Let's make ourselves ready!

Chapter 18

Stewarding the Wealth Transfer

Jesus recognized that men tended to be greedy. He even had one of His executive team pilfering the treasury of His ministry. If Jesus had that going on, we also might have similar issues.

It will be vital for you as a business owner to be sure that your business entity is a proper steward of the funds that come to it. In the previous chapter, we mainly dealt with the individual and their money handling. But as Kingdom Financiers, we must be extending those personal principles of tithes and offerings into our business so that we don't create any hindrance to the flow of funds. We can position our business for a solid financial flow by our giving or hesitancy in giving or see that flow cut off entirely.

We have to realize that, although we may need to calculate our giving differently than we would on a personal level, the business entity still needs to be giving.

In Proverbs, we find some incredible wisdom we need to implement in our lives and businesses.

Proverbs 11:23-31 says:

> *[23] The desire of the righteous is only good, But the expectation of the wicked is wrath.*
>
> *[24] There is one who scatters, yet increases more; and there is one who withholds more than is right, but it leads to poverty. [25] The generous soul will be made rich, and he who waters will also be watered himself. [26] The people will curse him who withholds grain, but blessing will be on the head of him who sells it. [27] He who earnestly seeks good finds favor, but trouble will come to him who seeks evil.*
>
> *[28] He who trusts in his riches will fall, but the righteous will flourish like foliage. [29] He who troubles his own house will inherit the wind, and the fool will be servant to the wise of heart.*
>
> *[30] The fruit of the righteous is a tree of life, and he who wins souls is wise.*
>
> *[31] If the righteous will be recompensed on the earth, how much more the ungodly and the sinner.*

This passage begins by speaking to the motivation of our heart which should be for good, not evil. Then it speaks of generosity. You have likely heard the testimony of people who are continuously giving and, as a result, are constantly flourishing. Giving is not limited to money. It covers many more areas.

Tithing

In my book *Building Your Business from Heaven Down 2.0*,[36] I share a synopsis of the various forms of giving. The first we usually call tithing, but tithing is not giving; it is returning. It is a stewarding for the Father to be returned to the assigned storehouse.

Offerings

Then we have offerings that are amounts above and beyond any tithe. If we have not tithed, God cannot bless it. The withholding of the tithe has an associated curse as one is robbing not the pastor, not the church congregation, not their family, not their friends. Rather, they are robbing God.[37] That is not a good position to be in.

Proverbs 26:2 tells us:

Like a flitting sparrow, like a flying swallow, So a curse without cause shall not alight.

If I don't want a curse to have the legal rights to land upon me or my business, I need to not qualify for that curse. Robbing God permits a curse to be placed upon them and their finances. The solution is simple: tithe and give offerings.

---

[36] *Building Your Business from Heaven Down 2.0*, LifeSpring Publishing (2020)
[37] Malachi 3:9

Firstfruits

Firstfruits are gifts unto the Lord in advance as seed for a coming harvest. Firstfruits should be commensurate with the expected harvest amount. If, for example, you want to sow a firstfruits for a $10,000 return, a $100 firstfruits seed is not equal with the desired harvest. Ask Heaven what the amount should be and respond accordingly.

Alms

Giving to the poor, widows, or orphans are examples of alms, but it is not limited to that. If, for example, you have a print shop and someone comes to you to get some printing done, but you need more time to service them well, you could recommend a competitor you know to do the job for them. That would be considered a giving of alms by you.

You could give someone a verbal recommendation, which is also a form of alms. Alms are much broader than we have believed.

In the Proverbs 11 passage that we have been reviewing, we find:

> *[25] The generous soul will be made rich, and he who waters will also be watered himself.*

Generosity will result in abundance. What you are giving, you will also receive. If I sow money, I will receive money. If I sow vehicles, I will receive vehicles. What we sow is what we reap. That is a fundamental principle of farming.

> ^{26} *The people will curse him who withholds grain, but blessing will be on the head of him who sells it.*

If you have a certain product and you withhold it without good cause, it will not generate goodwill for you and your business.

> ^{27} *He who earnestly seeks good finds favor, but trouble will come to him who seeks evil.*

Many times, what you need is not funds but favor. Favor will take you much farther than your money can. When you seek good and seek to do good, it will result in favor. The Old Testament contains the story of Job, who was tremendously blessed. Throughout the book of Job, you read of his good deeds, which resulted in blessings in his life. The calamity that Job faced lasted a long time, but actually, it was over from start to finish in just a few months or weeks. In the end, he was twice as blessed as he had been before.

Job was on Satan's radar because his blessing affected the economy of the land he lived in. Satan did not like the competition and took him to court. The only problem was that Job did not appear with him in court—not in chapters 1 or 2. His non-appearance resulted in default judgments placed upon him. However, Job triumphed through it all. As the next verse details, he was not guilty of trusting in his riches.

²⁸ He who trusts in his riches will fall, but the righteous will flourish like foliage. ²⁹ He who troubles his own house will inherit the wind, and the fool will be servant to the wise of heart.

³⁰ The fruit of the righteous is a tree of life, and he who wins souls is wise.

Your life and your business should produce fruit that is a tree of life—life-giving, not death-producing. Your business should have such qualities that Jesus could step in as CEO and have no discomfort with your business practices.

³¹ If the righteous will be recompensed on the earth, how much more the ungodly and the sinner.

Everyone will be recompensed.

---

*Remember, the seed you sow,
is the seed you grow.*

What kind of seed are you going to produce? What we do is a stewarding of what has come into our hands.

We must understand that all monies that come into our hands have an assignment. For example, last week, the twenty dollar bill in your wallet had the assignment to help buy some things for a little boy, pay for someone's lunch, or purchase gas for someone to travel to their next appointment. We should seek the Father concerning what the monies we are stewarding are assigned to do.

The money your employees receive as wages helps put food on their table and clothes on their backs. The purchase of that food helped pay the salaries of the farmers who produced the food, the workers in the grocery store, the wages of the truck driver who delivered it, and so on. It is a never-ending cycle of provision, so the money you are stewarding is not really yours. It is in trust to you. You have been entrusted with it.

Practice generosity. I know of people who give something to someone every day. They are creating a constant flow of money or whatever they are distributing into their lives and the lives of others.

Galatians 6:9 in the JB Phillips Translation says,

A man's harvest in life will depend entirely on what he sows. (Phillips)

What are you sowing? Can you do better? How well am I stewarding that which is in my hand?

As sons, the Father wants us to learn the basics, so we can be able to handle any influx that would come into our hands.

---
*When He can trust us,
we will be entrusted.*

Are we ready for it?

Chapter 19
Conclusion:
Governing as a Son

The intent of our heavenly Father is to unveil in us and through us, our sonship. He has sonship as our design. Many of us have struggled with embracing our sonship due to our religious (or non-religious) backgrounds; however, regardless of your history, your original blueprint was (and is) one of sonship unveiled in you and through you.

We are not the product of a religious system. Rather, we are becoming the sons the Father originally intended.

He did not design us to be victims
of circumstances or events.
Instead, he has made us victors.

Satan interfered with God's intent, and sin was introduced into our lives. A definition of sin is to live out of context with the blueprint of one's design, to behave out of tune with God's original harmony.

1 John 3:2 tells us, "Now we are the sons of God." It is not reserved for a future, far-off day. It is NOW! To advance your business as far as the Father desires, it will require you to step into your position as a legislative and judicial son of God. A son who knows who they are and whose they are. A son who understands that they are working from a mandate from Heaven and are working with and under the authority of Heaven. Sons are not content to let things happen. They will cause them to happen when needed. They will tap into the resources of Heaven to build what God has called them to build. *Que sera, sera*[38] is not our motto.

Rather, the latter portion of Daniel 11:32 will be their motto:

> *The people who know their God shall be strong,*
> *and carry out great exploits.*

We are not content to let things happen. We will make them happen as we follow the instructions of Heaven and live out of our scrolls and blueprints. We must develop our intimacy with the Father. We must rely on something other than old methods that were based in the Tree of the Knowledge of Good and Evil. If we are to build anything that lasts, we must build it from the knowledge that comes from the Tree of Life. Adam ate

---

[38] Que sera, sera, means "whatever will be will be." It was song sung by Doris Day in *The Man Who Knew Too Much* (1956).

from the wrong tree, but as sons, we can feast from the right tree—the Tree of Life. You have learned several things about your blueprint and your scroll. You have learned about your star and your business's star, the Spirit of Excellence, and your arche. Now it is time to put this information into practice.

In writing this book, I had to make certain assumptions. The first is that you had some familiarity with the things I teach concerning the Courts of Heaven, co-laboring with angels, engaging with men or women in white linen, and stepping into Heaven, among other things. I had to assume you were familiar with living spirit-forward or were at least willing to learn. I never try to convince someone concerning the things I write about. If they have ears to hear, they will hear. If not...next.

As you put these things into practice, you will be governing. You will be introducing the Kingdom of God into the earth.

> *And you shall remember the LORD your God, for it is He who gives you power to get wealth,* ***that He may establish His covenant*** *which He swore to your fathers, as it is this day. (Deuteronomy 8:18) (Emphasis added)*

God wants to establish
His covenant with you!

It's all about establishing His covenant in the earth. He did it with Adam, Noah, Abraham, and now He wants to do it with you. Will you let Him?

———·———

Appendix A

Accessing the Realms of Heaven

A tremendous privilege we share in this time in history is the ability to access the realms of Heaven with ease. Many of us were taught that Heaven is only for after you die. Heaven is much more than a final destination on a journey but also can be a vital aspect of that journey.

What I am about to share is vital in progressing in the various Courts of Heaven. We can access the Mercy Court in the Heavenly realm while fully planted here on the earth, but to maximize our endeavors in the Courts of Heaven, we need to learn how to operate FROM Heaven.

In teaching on accessing the realms of Heaven, I often point out some simple facts. If you were to tell me you were a citizen of a particular town, but you could tell me little of it from your personal experience, I would have a tendency to doubt the authenticity of your citizenship. I am a citizen of a small town in central North Carolina. I am familiar with the location of the city hall, police station, hospital, local county courthouse, Sheriff's Department, and much more. I know where many sporting events will be held. I know where the parks are. I know many of the stores and restaurants. I am familiar with this small town. Yet, if I were to ask the average believer what they can describe of Heaven from personal experience, the answer will likely be nothing. They have no personal experience of Heaven that they can relate to me. It does not have to be like that.

In Matthew 3, Jesus informed us that the Kingdom of Heaven was at hand. You could say, "The Kingdom of Heaven is as close as your hand." Hold your hand up in front of your nose as close as you could. Do not touch your nose. Heaven is closer to you than that. It is not far, far away up in the sky. It is not "over yonder" as some old hymns describe. It is a very present reality separated from us by a very thin membrane—and we can access it by faith. It is very simple.

When Jesus was baptized in the River Jordan, as He came up out of the water IMMEDIATELY the heavens were opened. He both saw (a dove) and heard (a voice coming from Heaven). This one act of Jesus restored our ability to access Heaven. We can experience open heavens over our life. We don't have to wait. We can live conscious of the realm of Heaven and live out of that reality!

---

*Everything we do as believers
we must do by faith.*

Accessing the realms of Heaven is done the same way. Prophetic acts can create realities for us. It is the same with this. You can visualize stepping from one room into another easily. It is like stepping from one place to another. To learn to access the realms of Heaven, you will follow the same pattern.

Stand up from where you are now and prepare to work with me. You can experience the realms of Heaven right now! You don't have to wait until you are dressed up in a long box at the local funeral home or decorating an urn. You can experience Heaven while you are alive! Remember, we enter the Kingdom as a child.

Quiet yourself down. Turn off distracting background noises if possible. Prepare to relax and focus. Now, say this with me:

> *Father, I would like to access the realms of Heaven today, so right now, by faith, I take a step into the realms of Heaven. [As you say that, take a step forward.] Imagine you are going from one place to another in a single step. Once you have done so, pay attention to what you see and hear. You may see very bright lights; you may see a river, a pastoral scene, a garden—any number of things. Right now, you are experiencing a taste of Heaven. You will notice the peace that pervades the atmosphere of Heaven. You might notice the air seems electric with life. The testimonies I've heard are always amazing and beautiful to hear.*

Now spend a few minutes in this place. Remember, Jesus said that to enter the Kingdom you must come as a little child. I often coach people to imagine yourself as an 8-year-old with what you are seeing. What would an 8-year-old do? He or she would be inquisitive and ask, "What is this? What does that do? Where does that go? Can I go here?" If a child saw a river or a lake, what would that child want to do? Most would want to jump in the water.

The variety is infinite. The colors—amazing! The sounds are so beautiful. You can learn to do this on a regular basis. When you access the realms of Heaven, you are home. You were made to experience the beauty that is Heaven.

The reason learning to access the realms of Heaven is crucial to engaging the Courts of Heaven is that much of what we do is done FROM Heaven. We need to learn to engage Heaven and work from it.

Many people tell me they can't "see" visually in the spirit. Often, they are discounting the ability they do have. They may be discounting their "knower." Every believer has a "knower" at work within them. This "knower" who is Holy Spirit at work within you helps you perceive things. Whether something is good or evil, He works to guide you more than you may have realized. Most navies that have submarines have a device known as sonar. Sonar gives a submarine "eyes" to see what is in their vicinity. They can detect what the object is by the ping emitted by the sonar. They can determine the distance to the object and if it is another submarine. They can even identify what class of submarine it might be. Sonar is invaluable in this setting, but a video camera would be rather useless underwater.

The military has a similar device for above ground situations known as radar. It functions in much the same manner. If a pilot were flying through thick cloud cover, the pilot would need to know what is in his path. Radar becomes his eyes.

Some people function visually. They often see what amounts to pictures or video images when they "see" in the spirit. They may see more detail. Yet one operating by his or her "knower" (their spiritual radar or sonar) can be just as effective as a seer. If you operate more like sonar or radar, don't discount what you "see" in that manner. It is how I function, and I have been doing this type of work for many years.

I can often detect where an angel is in the room (or if it is one of the men or women in white linen and not an angel). I can often detect how many are present and whether they have something they are to give to someone. I can detect any number of things and even though it is not "visual." it is still "seeing." It will set your mind at ease when you understand that operating by your knower is just as valid as any other type of vision. It will help you to realize you have been seeing much more than you know and you may know much more than some who only see.

Be willing to take a step right now into the realms of Heaven. You will be amazed at what you experience. You should sense a change in the atmosphere around you as well as sense the peace of God in an amazing manner. Enjoy the journey.

———·———

References

du Toit, F. (2022). *The Mirror Study Bible.* Mirror Word Publishing.

About the Author

Dr. Ron Horner is an apostolic teacher specializing in the Courts of Heaven. He has written nearly thirty books on the Courts of Heaven, engaging Heaven, working with angels, or living from revelation, as well as books on building your business from Heaven Down.

He also is CEO of Heaven Down Business, a worldwide consulting firm. He currently trains people in engaging the Courts of Heaven in a weekly online teaching session. You can register to participate and discover more about the Courts of Heaven prayer paradigm on his various websites, classes, products, and services found here:

www.ronhorner.com

_____ · _____

Description

Destiny Scrolls are like guideposts for the saints; they can map out the way Heaven sees something and how it could be built out. When following a Destiny Scroll, the best version of something can be achieved because it is the Father's will and His plan for that entity.

Blueprints are quantum maps of how a business will look in any place in time. They can be used in conjunction with the Destiny Scroll to ensure plans are being mapped out and executed correctly.

In this season, the Father is teaching His sons how to build businesses from Heaven Down. Learning how to perceive our Destiny Scrolls and blueprints is a crucial part of that process. This book will help unravel the mystery for you.

———·———

Other Books by Dr. Ron M. Horner

Building Your Business from Heaven Down

Building Your Business from Heaven Down 2.0

Building Your Business with the Blueprint of Heaven – Vol. 1

Commissioning Angels – Volume 1

Cooperating with The Glory

Courts of Heaven Process Charts

Dealing with Trusts & Consequential Liens

Engaging Angels in the Realms of Heaven

Engaging Heaven for Revelation – Volume 1

Engaging Heaven for Revelation – Volume 2

Engaging Heaven for Trade

Engaging the Courts for Ownership & Order

Engaging the Courts for Your City (*Paperback, Leader's Guide & Workbook*)

Engaging the Courts of Healing & the Healing Garden

Engaging the Courts of Heaven

Engaging the Help Desk of the Courts of Heaven

Engaging the Mercy Court of Heaven

Four Keys to Dismantling Accusations

Freedom from Mithraism

Let's Get it Right!

Lingering Human Spirits

Lingering Human Spirits – Volume 2

Living Spirit Forward

Overcoming the False Verdicts of Freemasonry

Overcoming Verdicts from the Courts of Hell

Releasing Bonds from the Courts of Heaven

Unlocking Spiritual Seeing

SPANISH

Cómo Proceder en la Corte Celestial de Misericordia

Las Cuatro Llaves para Anular las Acusaciones

Liberando Bonos en las Cortes Celestiales

Liberando Su Visión Espiritual

Sea Libre del Mitraísmo

Tablas de Proceso de la Cortes del Cielo

Viviendo desde el Espíritu

―――― · ――――

www.ingramcontent.com/pod-product-compliance
Lightning Source LLC
Chambersburg PA
CBHW022010160426
43197CB00007B/368